Wild Animal Care & Rehabilitation Manual

THIRD EDITION

By Patricia Adams & Vicki Johnson

Illustrated by Sharon Hartwigsen

Kalamazoo, Michigan

BEECH LEAF PRESS

Kalamazoo Nature Center, Inc.

1987

Additional copies may be obtained for $12.95 FROM:

BEECH LEAF PRESS
KALAMAZOO
Nature Center INC.
FOR
ENVIRONMENTAL EDUCATION
7000 N. Westnedge Avenue Kalamazoo, Michigan 49007
Telephone (616) 381-1574

U. S. A.

Publication of the first edition

of this manual was made possible by

the Michael E. Albert Memorial Wild Animal Care

and Rehabilitation Fund of the Kalamazoo Nature Center

First Printing, 1980

Second Printing, 1982

Second Edition, 1983

Third Edition, 1987

ISBN 0-939294-15-X

Library of Congress SF 997.A4b 1987

TABLE OF CONTENTS

INTRODUCTION

Everywhere we look, we see that people make impacts on the Earth--some beneficial and some harmful. In addition to injury, disease, and orphaning by nature's own hand, our wildlife suffers many problems caused by people. Besides destruction from loss of habitat and the harmful effects of toxic substances, wildlife suffers injury and orphaning because of vehicles, power lines, glass windows, irresponsible use of guns, lawn and garden cultivation, construction of various types, and for many other reasons.

In 1971, as an attempt to help compensate for these adverse effects on wildlife, the Kalamazoo Nature Center began its Wild Animal Care and Rehabilitation Program. Its major goal is to provide aid to injured and orphaned wildlife brought to the Center so that the animals may survive when released. Another important goal is to teach the public that, in general, it is better to leave wild animals in the wild unless it is known for certain that an animal is orphaned or injured. Included among the more than 15,000 individuals of over 50 species that have been rehabilitated and released into their natural habitats as a result of this program are: Bald and Golden Eagle; American Kestrel: Red-tailed Hawk; Barred, Eastern Screech-, Great Horned, and Long-eared owls; ducks; Green-backed Heron; many species of songbirds, shorebirds, and woodpeckers; opossums; raccoons; squirrels; Hoary Bat and Brown Bat; Gray and Red foxes; Badger; Striped Skunk; rabbits; various snakes and turtles; salamanders; and many more.

Primarily responsible for the success of this program to date are a number of dedicated wild animal care volunteers, who, after an 6-hour intensive training course at the Center, care for these animals at home. Volunteers raise the animals with the understanding that all will be returned to the wild and, therefore, must be prepared for survival in the natural world. The animals are fed natural foods as much as possible and kept outside as soon as they are old enough. Human contact is kept to a minimum so that the animals do not become pets. The overall success rate for the group is, at present, about 60%. Approximately 1,800 animals are brought to the Center each year.

During spring and summer, many types of "abandoned" wildlife are brought to the Nature Center. If, after talking with those who bring young animals to the Center, it is felt that a particular animal was not orphaned, but merely temporarily out on its own, the individual is asked to take the animal back where it was found, to release it, and to stay out of the area so that the parent can relocate the "baby."

Some animals are, of course, orphaned, and these are cared for in the program. A 2-session course is offered during April, where interested individuals learn how to raise and prepare wildlife for release. Habits, natural foods, substitute formulas for milk, proper confinement and warmth, temporary first aid, and other necessities are learned. Major emphasis is placed on setting up the raising and releasing of animals, utilizing knowledge of the natural history of each species every step of the way. All approved animal care volunteers function under the Nature Center's educational and wildlife rehabilitation permits from the Michigan Department of Natural Resources and receive a special Nature Center permit for each animal they care for. Many volunteers have kept logs of animals raised and special techniques used, thus contributing to the substance of this manual.

Knowing how to release an animal is as important as knowing how to raise it. Observation of what occurs in nature provides the most helpful hints for release. Songbirds, for example, are seen feeding together in family groups for 1-3 weeks after the young have left the nest, perhaps insuring that the young learn a wide variety of food sources and survival skills from the parents. Young hawks and owls stay with the adults well into summer, influencing the development of hunting techniques. Raccoon, opossum, squirrel, and other mammal families may stay together until late summer or early fall, allowing the young to learn as much about food sources, shelter, and safety as possible.

Because of the program's goal of insuring survival in the wild of those animals that have received so much care, some animals are released from volunteers' homes, and others are returned to Nature Center property or are taken to other protected areas for release. Platforms may be erected or a cage with food may be left out for a gradual "weaning" of the animal being

4

released. Songbirds usually return to these "home" feeding platforms regularly for food, especially for the first 1-2 weeks. Hawks and owls may take 2 months or more before they are able to hunt their own food sufficiently to survive. Raccoons may be taken to wild places and often are placed in special "release pens" with other raccoons away from human contact, fed natural foods for 2-3 weeks and released, in some cases with the help of conservation officers. In other cases raccoons are transported to good release sites and released with a food supply placed under a wood structure to protect food from the elements. The release program is tailored to fit each species of animal. Factors such as weather, territory, and safety are considered before an animal is released. Without such careful attention to detail, the survival rate of animals raised by humans and released would be low.

All formulas, tips, and other information in this manual have been tested by Kalamazoo Nature Center volunteers over the past 15 years. In the sections on birds and mammals, the warming and re-hydration procedures are re-stated for each animal. This is done so that each section can be used separately.

In addition, new information has been added to the chapters on Opossoms, Raccoons, Badgers, Foxes, Deer, Altricial Birds, and Precocial Birds. New chapters have been added: Muskrats, Green-backed Herons, Belted Kingfishers, and How We Operate Our Program.

This manual has been written primarily for Kalamazoo Nature Center Wild Animal Care and Rehabilitation Volunteers. However, it is hoped that it may be useful to other wildlife rehabilitation groups, nature centers, zoos, humane societies, and others interested in aiding our wildlife. Comments and suggestions will be appreciated. Please send them to the Kalamazoo Nature Center Wildlife Rehabilitation Program, 7000 North Westnedge Avenue, Kalamazoo, Michigan 49007 (telephone 616-381-1574).

ACKNOWLEDGMENTS

We give special thanks to our veterinarians, Dr. Charles Mehne and Dr. William Gregg, for their kindness and devotion to the animals and to the Rehabilitation Program over the years. Grateful thanks are given to Dr. H. Lewis Batts, Jr., for his editorial contributions, and to Monica Evans for her efforts in helping to bring this manual to completion. Special thanks to volunteers Pixie Goodrich, Rae Haas, and Bob Fleshman for their contributions from the vast storehouse of their experience in the production of the third edition of this manual. Deep appreciation is extended to the dedicated volunteers who make this program possible.

SUCCESS-FAILURE

Successfully raising young animals or nursing injured or sick animals to the point of being able to fend for themselves in the natural world is a most rewarding and useful experience.

However, do not expect 100% success. If, in spite of all you do for an animal, it dies, do not give up or get discouraged. You have given the animal a chance that it may never have had in the wild. You have also learned some valuable information which can be used to benefit the lives of future animals you will raise and release. In nature 50%-60% of all young animals do not survive the first year. You have helped those who might have died early to have a second chance.   Remember, you are not a mother wild animal, only a substitute, so you will not know all that a mother animal will know about raising her young. You are trying, learning, and growing with each experience, and your success rate will increase as you raise more animals. Much can be gained by sharing this philosophy with other members of your family.

IF YOU HAVE TO
DISPOSE OF AN ANIMAL

Occasionally there will be a need to put an animal out of its misery. Animals may be severely ill, injured, or otherwise unsalvageable. Under these circumstances it is advisable to end suffering and there are several ways to do this.

The decision to dispose of an animal should be made as objectively as possible. If an animal can be treated and cured to survive in a healthy manner and without pain or hardship in the wild (or in captivity if proper facilities are available), it should be helped. Animals that are incurable or would survive only with pain and difficulty should not be kept alive because of emotional attachment.

The best method is to use injections with any of several death-causing agents. Consult with your supervisor or veterinarian for the proper equipment and dosages. This method is the quickest and most painless, often involving only 3-6 seconds, depending on the size of the animal, the chemical used, and route administered.

The Nature Center also utilizes a CO_2 chamber. The chamber is a 4' long, 2' high, 2' wide wooden box, tightly constructed. There is a glass window built into the top of the chamber for observation. The CO_2 tank is connected by valves and a hose to one end of the chamber. The top is attached to the box by a hinge and may be clamped shut. Varying amounts of CO_2 enter the chamber, depending on the size of the animal. The animal is left in the chamber for 5 minutes after the gas is turned off to ensure that it is dead before disposal.

If these methods are not available, there are some others which can be used in the home.

Method A
Drowning an animal in a sink, tub, or bucket will put it out of its misery.

Method B

Place the animal in an airtight bag and tie the end of the bag over the exhaust pipe of a car, then turn on the engine. With smaller animals, death can occur fairly quickly; with larger animals, it can take 20-30 minutes. However, this is likely painless and can be preferable to prolonged suffering on the part of the animal or danger to you or your family from disease.

Method C

Although it may sound harsh, quickly breaking an animal's neck is an effective way to dispose of it.

With larger animals (deer, adult raccoon, fox, badger, etc.), you may ask your local conservation officer to come and dispose of it by shooting. Another possibility is to take the larger animal to the local animal control facility and ask personnel there to dispatch it.

IMPRINTING

Imprinting, according to one definition, is the process of "impressing upon the heart or mind." In wild animals this process is one by which the young animal identifies with the adult of its own species and learns by imitation and observation the methods for finding food, shelter, safety, and means of survival including aggressive, submissive, mating, and defensive behaviors.

If care is not taken, the process of imprinting can be transferred to the human who raises and releases young wild animals. If young wild animals become permanently imprinted on humans or dogs or cats, they should not be released--they will have a poor chance for survival. Animals that do not imprint on their own species will lack survival skills, including proper mating behaviors, good territorial/defensive behaviors, proper skills and instructions for finding food and shelter, and a place in the social hierarchy of their own species. Often those that do not imprint on their own kind are either killed outright by their own or other species or shoved to less desirable and productive habitats where they may eventually starve. Or they may continually return to humans for food causing them to become garbage-can pests or to be shot as "chicken hawks or owls" or misjudged as diseased animals.

Precautions must be taken so that the animals imprint on their own species and not on humans.

SOME HELPFUL SUGGESTIONS

If at all possible, raise an animal with at least one other member of its own species. Raise raccoons with raccoons, hawks with the same species of hawk, squirrels with like species of squirrels, rabbits with rabbits, songbirds with the same species of songbirds, etc. Also, animals placed together should be about the same age unless they are family groups. For example, after they become 3-4 weeks old, young ducklings put in with older ducklings often will be harrassed or pecked to death. Mammals markedly older than other mammals in the same cage may monopolize the food supply and optimum cage space.

Handle animals as little as possible. Handling during feeding and cleaning when animals are very young is necessary. However, after these chores are completed, the animals should be returned to the box and left alone, so that they will play together and learn social behaviors from each other rather than develop a dependence on humans for their social needs.

When feeding or cleaning, try to appear and sound as much like the adult of the species as possible. With raptors and songbirds particularly, it is a good idea to try to imitate food calls or small sounds the bird may make to locate the adult for contact. To help with proper imprinting, try to locate a stuffed adult of the same species and place it in or near the cage so that it is visible to the youngsters. Or when possible, place the young animal's cage or box next to or near adult captive birds of the same species. Some rehabilitators have found success by using mirrors. The birds imprint on themselves through their reflections in the mirror. Also, tape recordings of most bird songs should be played close to the birds so they will learn their own songs. This is particularly important for male song birds so that they may be prepared for the breeding season the next year.

Study, by reading or direct observation, the natural habits and behavior of the animals you are raising. Be scientifically creative in attempts to keep the animals from identifying with humans. For example, one well-known raptor rehabilitator feeds young hawks and owls with the skin of an adult of the same species draped over the hand placing the food in the mouth of the young or in the cage. This helps to imprint the young visually on one of its kind, and to associate food with its own species rather than with humans.

Most animals are more susceptible to imprinting within the first 10 days to 2 weeks after they open and focus their eyes. It is particularly important to take extra precautions against imprinting on humans at this critical time, although caution should be exercised during the entire first 3 months of existence.

MAMMALS

GENERAL INFORMATION

SUPPLIES AND EQUIPMENT NEEDED

1. Heating pad and 60-watt light bulb
2. Cages and boxes of various sizes (cottage cheese cartons, berry boxes, cardboard boxes) for young mammals
3. Soft rags, towels (not terry cloth), diapers, flannel, old T-shirts, or facial tissue
4. Food: Esbilac or Unilact for babies; natural food for older animals
5. Plastic eye-dropper, syringe, nursing bottle, coffee stirrers, spoon handles
6. Gloves: a pair to be worn when feeding raccoons; a heavier pair to wear when handling older animals
7. Thermometer
8. Hydrogen peroxide, gauze, Q-tips, cat flea powder, A & D ointment
9. Log book
10. Large outdoor cages to prepare the animals for release
11. Natural history books

ENVIRONMENT

1. Chilling is the single greatest danger, but overheating and dehydration can also produce many problems.
2. Maintain proper temperatures--95°-100°F for very young.
3. Use container lined with flannel, other soft rags, facial tissue, or diapers. Do not use cotton. Make sure animals can't get out. Change size of box as animal grows.
4. Place a heating pad under 1/4-1/3 of the box and up one side--allowing warmth when needed but escape to a cooler portion of the box if the animal is too warm. Adjust heating pad so box is warm--not hot.
5. If a light bulb is used as a heat source, place the bulb close enough

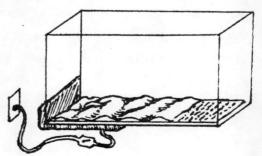

to give the animals adequate warmth but not so close that they could jump or climb onto the bulb and be burned. The bulb should be moved farther away as the animals develop fur. When the animals require less artificial heat, they will position themselves away from the warmest areas.

6. Make certain housing is cleaned twice daily or more often if necesary.

FEEDING

1. During the first few days of an infant's life, its mother's milk contains colostrum, which is extremely high in protein and carries much of the disease immunity necessary to the young. Newborn animals denied the chance to nurse from the mother are extremely difficult to raise and require very specialized care and diet.

2. Use Esbilac or Unilact and mix as directed in manual for one day at a time. Formula should be fed at 100°F or should feel warm to the inside of your wrist. Use plastic eye-dropper, nursing bottle, or syringe.

3. Just before feeding, a regular gentle massage of the skin stimulates circulation and thoroughly awakens the animal.

4. Feed every 2-4 hours or as the manual suggests, until the young are full--the belly should be firm to the touch but not rigid--usually 2-3 eye-droppersfull at first and then increasing.

5. Feed animals in their normal nursing position, prone--not on their backs.

6. Elimination of waste must be stimulated after each feeding by gently stroking belly and anal areas with a warm moist cloth, keeping this up until flow stops. Discontinue stimulation after about a minute, whether or not the animal has eliminated. This must be done until the animal's

13

eyes are completely open or it is eliminating on its own. Hold over a sink or newspaper.

7. If diarrhea occurs, one of the following diet changes may be made. If the diarrhea continues for more than 24-30 hours after trying one of these methods, call your supervisor or veterinarian.

   a) Dilute the basic formula with water. For example, mix one part Esbilac or Unilact with 5 or 6 parts water.

   b) Alternate regular feedings with a solution of flat cola (let the "fizz" leave the cola) or other re-hydration solution.

   c) Put animal on Pedialyte for 24 hours and reintroduce regular formula slowly if diarrhea has lessened.

8. If bloat occurs, skip a feeding or 2, place the abdomen in warm water and massage for 4-5 minutes. Do not chill animal.

9. Feces should be carefully watched for signs of parasites, lack of fat (large globs of white) absorption, and other abnormal bodily functions. Always be on the lookout for blood in the feces, a sure sign of major intestinal dysfunction or infection. Call your supervisor or veterinarian if this occurs.

10. Make sure the animals eat and are growing steadily. Weighing the animals daily will confirm a steady weight gain.

11. Feed weaned animals during the time they would naturally feed in the wild. Some animals feed during the day, but many, such as raccoons, owls, fox, and muskrats feed mostly at night.

WEANING

Weaning is usually accomplished by gradually replacing formula with natural foods. Weaning usually starts as the eyes open and teeth begin to appear. Weaning can last from 1-3 weeks depending on the age and species of animal.

Mammals have a strong natural nursing reflex and will suck on their own genitals and those of their litter mates.   This can cause uremic poisoning in some mammals, especially in the weasel family. To help them stop sucking the genital area, wash this area with a mild soap, leaving some of the soap on, or place A & D ointment on the genital area. In some cases it may be necessary to wait until the animal outgrows this habit.

RELEASE

Begin planning for the animals' release the day they are received into the rehabilitation program. Read as much as you can about how your species exists in the wild--the habitat, food, unique behaviors, etc. The more you know, the better you'll be able to prepare the animals for release.

The process of rehabilitating young animals is not complete until the animals have been released into their natural habitats and allowed every consideration for survival without you. Releasing animals does not mean simply letting them go. Animals must be prepared as completely as possible if they are to have a fair chance of making it.

As you are preparing your animals for release, always consider whether or not you are teaching them anything that will be detrimental to them in the wild. For example, you may be seriously handicapping your wild animals if you always feed them from a dish. When released, they will undoubtedly be unsuccessful in locating food if they have learned to look for it in a dish. You should present natural foods in as natural a setting as possible (e.g., greens should be placed on soil, not in a dish). Another example: if your animals are allowed access to the family dog, you are teaching the wild animals that dogs are not a danger. Keep your wild animals away from your dog and/or cat. The young animals learn their survival skills from the mother--in the absence of the mother, it's your job to equip them with as many of these skills as you can. Don't teach anything that will inhibit their chances of survival in the wild without you.

The animals must be physically as well as mentally prepared. This means that they must not acquire attachments, such as a dependency on you as a care-giver. They should be physically fit--healthy, well-furred, eating a balanced diet of natural foods, and have lived outside in the elements (day and night, rain and shine). If the animals depend on catching prey to survive, you must provide the opportunity to do this. This means, in some cases, that you will have to supply live prey so the predators can learn how to hunt. And in all cases, they must have eaten in captivity what they will eat in the wild. It is imperative that you study the natural life of the animals in order to know what their needs will be in the wild.

In selecting a release site, there are some questions you need to ask. Does this release site provide these animals with appropriate food, water, den or nesting possibilities, and cover? Are there others of the same species living in this habitat? If there are others, is there enough land, food, etc. to support the additional animals? Is this release area far enough away from human populations and roads? What is the predator situation? Is hunting, trapping, or camping allowed on this property? (Are you merely supplying targets, for example?) Is there possibility of chemical contamination?

Properly prepared animals cannot make it if the habitat is unsuitable; the best possible habitat won't do unprepared animals any good. Without both--a properly prepared animal and suitable habitat--an animal's chances of survival are greatly reduced.

CHECKLIST FOR PROBLEM-SOLVING

1. Is feeding-bottle rinsed clear of all detergents and stale formula?
2. Have you tried alternate feeding apparatus--eye-dropper, bottle, syringe?
3. Did you change foods suddenly?
4. Any stress?   (Temperature change, draft, strangers around, dog or cat, screaming or other loud noises, chilled, over-heated, etc.)
5. Did you use cow's milk?
6. Was formula fresh? Is water fresh?
7. Is cage dirty?
8. Any sharp wires or nails around?
9. Possibility of disease?   Labored breathing, discharge from nose or mouth? Other signs?
10. Have you recently placed another animal in the cage?

SPECIAL WARNINGS

1. Make sure young are growing and healthy--examine stools and feel body cavity (should be plump and firm).
2. Use no aerosols in the room.
3. If you must leave the animals with a "baby sitter," use a trained person.
4. Watch for access to open water (kitchen sink, toilet, etc.).
5. Watch for hot stoves.
6. Do not use stringy cloth covers in or on cages.
7. Work low over the floor or on a large table to prevent injury from falling.
8. Be careful with vacuum cleaners.
9. Protect from cats and dogs.
10. Do not make pets of wild animals.
11. Do not overfeed.
12. Do not teach animals to find food in a dish.
13. Do not raise animals alone--try to raise them in groups of 2 or more.
14. Check carefully to be sure your outside cages are predator-proof.

People raising animals should have a regular tetanus shot and those who work with possible carriers of rabies should be aware of the symptoms and effects of the disease. There is a special rabies shot that can be given to protect those working with high-incidence rabies carriers. If at all possible, people working with animals susceptible to rabies should be vaccinated with pre-immunization rabies shots (available, hopefully from your local public health department or doctor for a reasonable cost).

FIRST AID FOR MAMMALS

DON'T TRY TO BE AN AMATEUR DOCTOR--BE A GOOD ANIMAL CARETAKER

**WARNING: WHEN TREATING ANY INJURY, AVOID BITES AND SCRATCHES--THE BEHAVIOR
OF AN ANIMAL IN FRIGHT OR PAIN IS UNPREDICTABLE.**

MAGGOTS

Clip hair around infested area carefully; most infestations are larger than
they look.   Remove maggots from on or in the skin with Q-tips or tweezers
dipped in medical hydrogen peroxide (not hair bleach).   When all maggots are
removed, apply sulfa-urea or other recommended dressing with a Q-tip twice
daily until healing is complete.

FLEAS AND TICKS

Make sure of the identification before treating.   A tick-dip solution is
available from vets and works very well (Paramite or VIP dip solution) or use
VIP Flea and Tick Powder or **cat** flea powder as directed on the container.
Ticks may have to be removed manually.   Use tweezers, grip the tick as close
to its head as possible, and pull very slowly straight out.   Do not turn it.
Occasionally a tick's head may stay in the animal's skin.   Apply hydrogen
peroxide until it pops out.   Heat or salt applied directly to the **tick only**
will cause it to back out, thus removing itself.

MINOR CUTS, LACERATIONS, AND WOUNDS

Stop any bleeding with adequate pressure, using a gauze pad, and clean the
wounds.   This usually involves removing hair in the area and washing with a
mild soap or cleaning with hydrogen peroxide.

SEVERE OR DEEP CUTS

Apply pressure with gauze or a clean washcloth (do not use absorbent cotton)
above and below the wound and seek professional help immediately.

FALLS, CONCUSSIONS, ETC.

Seek help immediately, especially if gums are pale (indicating internal bleeding or shock). Keep the animal as quiet as possible, avoid excitement, and keep warm.

BROKEN BONES

Place the animal in a box to avoid movement. Do NOT try to set broken bones--seek professional help.

BURNS, HEATSTROKE, ETC.

Keep the animal quiet, place it in a container, and call your supervisor or veterinarian.

URINE RASH OR FECAL BURNS

Wash off and apply Vitamin A and D ointment.

VACCINATIONS

The Kalamazoo Nature Center vaccinates all the foxes and racoons that it releases. Vaccinations are given for rabies and several forms of distemper.

There is some dispute as to the effectiveness of using canine and feline distemper vaccinations for wild animals. Currently there are attempts being made in various locations in the country to develop special raccoon distemper vaccines. It is unknown whether the parvo-virus vaccines are effective in wild animals. Any animal receiving rabies vaccinations should always receive **only** "killed" vaccine, never "live" vaccine. Live rabies vaccine may actually cause rabies in the animal. Most vaccines, if effective, will protect the animal's system for only one year.

Recent information from some wildlife vets with training in pathology indicates that it is sometimes difficult to determine whether a sick animal actually may have distemper. The incubation period may be several months. Also, the diseased cells may react differently within different tissues of the animal. Several parts of the animal's body should be checked thoroughly for symptoms of disease as opposed to checking only 1 area.

DISEASES OF MAMMALS

If you suspect that an animal is diseased, consult your supervisor immediately and a veterinarian will be consulted.

RABIES

At its highest levels, it is present in about 5% of the population of species which can carry rabies. The disease travels through the nervous system to the brain (behavior patterns depend on portion of brain involved). Research indicates that the sense of taste is distorted, the throat is paralyzed, and animals may be drooling or dazed. Few animals become actually aggressive, most retreat and die. It is a viral disease and all warm-blooded animals are susceptible. Bats and skunks are suspected to be permanent hosts of the virus. Rabies generally is divided into 2 groups, canine rabies and wild rabies; canine is on the decline and wild is on the increase. Foxes, raccoons, skunks, and bats are the most common carriers; foxes are the most susceptible. Incubation from time of exposure varies from 10 days to 6 months, with cases over 1 year in skunks; both "dumb" and "furious" rabies may result. Hydrophobia is not present in most animals.

SALMONELLA

Salmonella bacteria cause paratyphoid, enteritis, ptomaine, and other intestinal diseases primarily because of a lack of proper care in preparation of food and cleaning of pens. Some forms are transmitted to people, usually as enteritis accompanied by high fever.

TULAREMIA

Tularemia is a bacterial plague-like disease of wild rabbits, hares, and rodents, which can be transmitted through contamination of the environment, direct contact, arthropods, and ectoparasites. Found in 48 species of birds and mammals--rabbits are responsible for 80-90% of human infection--usually contracted from handling a carcass or live animal, or from insect vectors such as flies and ticks. Signs are not always visible, but rabbits often

21

move slowly and are easily caught--appear to be tame or in a stupor, do not raise their heads well, rub noses and forefeet into the ground, exhibit spasms and some diarrhea and labored breathing. Human infection includes local lesions with ulceration, headaches, body aches and fever; the disease runs its course in 2-4 weeks; its fatality rate is 5%. Treatment includes tetracycline or streptomycin, to both of which bacteria can build up resistance rapidly. The disease is almost always fatal in wild populations.

DISTEMPER

This is a viral disease to which members of canine, weasel, and raccoon groups are most susceptible. It may be related to measles in humans in form, treatment, and symptoms. Transmission is by aerosol or direct contact and produces much nasal and conjuctival exudate in infected animals. Little is actually known about distemper in wild populations even though signs include watery eyes, reddening of skin in head and anal areas, swelling of foot pads, and marked fever, with drops to subnormal temperature before death. Raccoons also show neurological disturbances, convulsive movements, and aimlessness. Incubation ranges from 8-20 days; death in 50-75% of animals comes within 3 weeks of infection.

Recent information from some wildlife vets with training in pathology indicates that it is sometimes difficult to determine whether a sick animal actually may have distemper. The incubation period may be several months. Also, the diseased cells from differing parts and tissues of the animal react differently within an animal's system. Lab studies should include tissue samples from a variety of locations within the diseased animal.

ARBOVIRUSES

These viruses are arthropod-borne and cause about 200 encephalitis-type diseases. Most infected animals can be treated if detected early enough, although some forms are always fatal. Most cannot be transmitted from infected animals; the arthropod route may be a source of human infection.

FELINE DISTEMPER (Panleukipenia)

This disease mainly affects members of the cat family; raccoons can be hosts. Mink viral enteritis is very similar and can accompany feline distemper--fleas and house flies serve as vectors. Signs include sudden

22

onset of depression, fever, vomiting, diarrhea--vomit is often a bile-stained mixture of mucus and gastric juices; feces are bloody. Mortality is 60-90%.

MYXOMATOSIS

An insect-transmitted pox-virus disease of rabbits. First signs are lesions on extremeties, skin red and thickened, watery secretion from eyes and nose. Death usually results in 8-12 days. There is no effective treatment; antibiotics are useless. Squirrels and woodchucks usually are victims.

INFECTIOUS CANINE HEPATITIS (ICH)

This virus causes hepatitis in dogs and encephalitis in foxes, raccoons, mink, and ferrets. It spreads by contact with infected animals or contaminated materials. Symptoms appear suddenly after incubation of from 2-6 days; first sign of illness is loss of appetite, soft feces streaked with blood, and hemorrhage into lumen of bowel. It is usually fatal; animals which survive are generally immune.

SYLVATIC PLAGUE

One of 6 internationally quarantinable diseases, the sylvatic plague is spread by fleas of rodent hosts and may be transmitted to humans. Real danger comes from an infected human who develops "pneumonic" form of the disease. It is present in many squirrels and rabbits.

MANGE

Mange is the loss of hair from an animal, caused by a small mite on the skin. Mites also may work themselves down into the skin causing cracks or flaking in the skin layer. Mange appears to occur most frequently in squirrels and foxes. For animals half-grown or older, one method of treatment is to wash or dip the animal thoroughly in Mycodex or a good commercial flea and tick shampoo. The dip or shampoo should be kept on for 5 minutes before rinsing. Treatment should be repeated daily for 3 days. For some adult animals, it should be repeated 1-2 weeks after the first treatment. Consult the directions on the product. Keep out of eyes, nose, mouth. Cage and bedding should be completely changed and new housing dusted with cat flea and tick powder to prevent re-infestation.

Very young animals having mange must be treated with caution. The chemical pesticides in the dip or shampoo solutions may be able to cause spinal cord and nerve damage. Consult a veterinarian. Nature Center volunteers have tried 2 remedies: 1) a very dilute solution of dip or shampoo is applied less frequently than for adults. Do not chill animal. 2) Lime sulfate solution seems to work better for younger animals. This solution, which has a very strong odor, must be applied once a day for 3 days. Do not chill the animal or get solution into eyes, nose, or mouth. Completely change bedding. Apply cat flea and tick powder to new bedding.

For treatment of mature squirrels with mange, a single dose of injectable ivermectin (specifically "Ivomec") is effective. A second dose can be given 3-4 weeks later if and only if needed. Please consult your veterinarian for this treatment.

PASTEURELLOSIS

This infectious bacterial disease produces hemorrhaging; it takes the form of pneumonia, arthritis, mastitis, meningitis, and blood poisoning. It has been found in bison, deer, chipmunks, elk, mink, muskrats, rabbits, raccoons, and weasels. Bacteria seem to be always present in the upper respiratory tract of mammals and increase enough to cause problems when an animal's system experiences reduced food supply, weakness, stress, etc. Contamination is through saliva and feces. Onset of the disease is rapid. Signs are few, although emaciation, nasal and eye discharge, and motor impairment are present. Prognosis for animals with acute or subacute forms is very poor; animals with the chronic form may recover.

WHAT TO DO FIRST

Some animals will come to you warm and healthy, and they will be ready to be fed and housed; others will come in chilled, down-right cold, or dehydrated. The first task is to get their body temperature up. Do NOT feed cold or chilled animals for they cannot digest food properly and may die from using up the last remaining energy trying to do so. Most birds and mammals have body temperatures of 95°F or higher (birds are generally higher).

To warm the animals: use your hands; hold the animals under your shirt next to your body; use a heating pad on low (covered with cloths or diapers, or placed under the box); or hang a 60-watt light bulb over the animals at a proper distance. The animals should not be warmed too quickly--they may die of hyperthermia if the outer layer of flesh warms too rapidly for the inner, colder layers to supply them with needed blood-warmth and oxygen. If you use a heating pad or light bulb, leave room for the animals to get away to a cooler part of the box or cage when warmed. For example, place the box on half of the pad, leaving one side cooler.

After the animals are warmed, determine if they are dehydrated. A combination of observations may help you. The animals are dehydrated if they are thin, weak, or listless; and if, after the skin of the animals is lightly pinched between your thumb and index finger, it stays up (tents). Two home-made re-hydration solutions and 4 commercial pre-mixed solutions for human babies (available from most pharmacies) may be useful.

RE-HYDRATING

Solution #1	Solution #2	4 Commercial Solutions
Warm 3 tablespoons	1 teaspoon salt	Warm Pedialyte or
of a flat cola drink	3 tablespoons sugar	Gatorade or
with 1 teaspoon of honey	1 quart warm water	Normosol R or
		Lactated Ringers

Feed dehydrated animals every 15-30 minutes or so with an eye-dropper, being careful not to get any solution down air tubes or lungs. The amount will vary depending upon the size of the animals--a few drops for a newborn bunny or several eye-droppersful for a raccoon. Keep the animals warm and when they are re-vitalized, start feeding them formula.

If the animals have been unusually cold, remain listless, and don't feed well, it may be a good idea to give antibiotics for a day or two. Do not do this without the advice of a supervisor or a veterinarian. Antibiotics may be available free from some pharmaceutical companies. Our supply is donated. Call the Animal Rehabilitation office to make the necessary arrangments. A general rule to follow is about 1 drop of general antibiotic per ounce of body weight, given every 4-7 hours for 2-3 days at most.

Do not place animals in air-conditioned rooms or rooms with drafts. Do not subject animals to sudden or significant temperature changes.

There are a number of diseases which animals can get, so if animals show symptoms of a disease, contact a supervisor to make an appointment with a veterinarian.

All animals should be thoroughly examined when received. If signs of broken bones, sprains, muscle problems, paralysis, etc., are present, contact a supervisor to make an appointment with a veterinarian. Attempts are made at the Nature Center when the animals come in to screen for complications so that volunteers do not receive animals with severe problems.

———

The next 12 chapters describe our experiences with these mammals:

Opossoms	Badgers	Woodchucks	Muskrats
Bats	Skunks	Squirrels	Rabbits
Raccoons	Foxes	Mice	Deer

OPOSSUMS

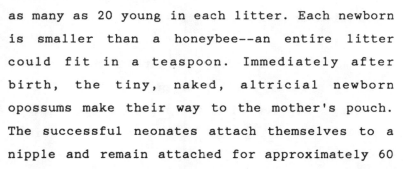

IN THE WILD

Opossums, the only
marsupial in North
America, may have
as many as 20 young in each litter. Each newborn
is smaller than a honeybee--an entire litter
could fit in a teaspoon. Immediately after
birth, the tiny, naked, altricial newborn
opossums make their way to the mother's pouch.
The successful neonates attach themselves to a
nipple and remain attached for approximately 60
days. At about 2 months of age, the young are furred and spend some time
outside the pouch. The mother's nipples will now allow the young to lie
outside the pouch while suckling. At about 70 days, the young opossums will
leave the mother and crawl short distances before returning to the pouch.
Sometime around the 87th day, weaning begins. The young will show an
interest in solid food but are still suckling. At this point, the young
accompany the mother when she forages--either running along beside or riding
on her back. Over the next week, the young will increase their intake of
solid food as they decrease the amount of milk they take from their mother.
By the 104th day, all young are weaned and are largely independent of their
mother.

Opossums prefer deciduous woodlands near small streams. However, they seem
to be able to adapt to various habitats, such as marshlands and agricultural
areas as well as suburban habitats. Opossums are not territorial and don't
maintain separate home ranges. They are generally solitary wanderers that
rarely remain in any one area for long periods of time.

Opossums are omnivorous and will eat almost anything. They may scavenge
carrion as well as eat quantities of grass and other green vegetation. They
will eat other birds and mammals, crayfish, bird eggs, frogs, worms, corn,

wild grapes, and buckwheat. About 65% of their diet consists of mammals (most of which is probably carrion) and 35% consists of plant material.

WHAT TO DO FIRST

When you receive young opossums, try to determine their age, and how they were found. If the babies are from the pouch of a dead mother, you can assume that you will have a low survival rate because these animals aren't fully formed. The very young are practically transparent. Your success will increase if they are slightly furred and fully formed. See special note at the end of this section for information on raising hairless embryos.

If the opossums do not feel warm, it is necessary to get the temperature back to normal. This can be done by putting the litter on a warm hot water bottle wrapped in towels. A heating pad covered with towels or clean rags, or your own body heat can be used. A heating pad should warm the animal slowly--don't let the temperature get hot.

If the skin tents when gently pinched and the opossums seem listless and weak, they are probably dehydrated. After the animals regain their normal body temperature, they should be given a small drink of re-hydrating solution every 15 minutes over the first hour. The amount of solution will depend on the size of the animal. Re-hydration solution: 1 tsp. salt, 3 tbs. sugar in 1 quart warm water.

If you are sure the opossums are warm and hydrated, proceed to prepare housing and begin normal feeding schedule.

HOUSING

Line any small box with newspaper and then add flannel or towelling. The sides of the box must be high enough so that the opossums can't climb out.

If a heating pad is used, place the pad outside and under 1/4 to 1/3 of the box and up one side. This allows warmth when needed but escape if it is too warm. Start the pad on low heat and use your hand to feel the warmth coming through the box--it should feel warm, not hot. The temperature for the very young should be 95°F. The size and depth of the box should be adjusted as the opossums become more mobile. Opossums are messy and need to have their bedding and newspapers changed often. When they are fully furred, remove heating devices and begin taking the animals outside on warm days. Bring them in at night until they are at least half grown.

FEEDING

Use 1 part Esbilac or Unilact to 3 parts warm water. Add 3-4 drops of pet vitamins to each cup of formula. The warm formula can be fed to the opossums using an eyedropper, a syringe or a pet-nurser.

Before beginning to feed be sure the opossums are fully awake. Sometimes it is helpful to gently massage the animals until they appear fully awake and alert. This massaging action simulates the mother animal licking her babies before they begin to nurse.

If the young are healthy and eating well, feed them approximately every 4 hours. If the animals are weak or not eating well, they may have to be fed more often until they regain their strength and begin eating vigorously.

Usually the young will stop sucking when they are full. Their stomachs will be round and firm when full--not tight or bloated. It is just as unhealthy to overfeed young as it is to underfeed them.

Following each feeding, rub the belly and genital areas with a warm, damp cloth. This usually stimulates the young to urinate or have a bowel movement; but don't worry if it doesn't work every time. Discontinue the stimulation after a minute whether or not they have eliminated. This activity can be discontinued altogether once the animals begin to eliminate on their own without stimulation. You'll know this has occurred when you see droppings and urine in the box. Each infant should be independent of this stimulation by the time the eyes have opened.

When the eyes have opened (sometime between the 58th and 72nd days), begin offering them natural food. They probably won't eat much but will begin to get used to the smell of solid diet. The opossums will begin showing an interest in solid food by about the 87th day and will start nibbling on fruit or greens. Continue to offer the formula until they are able to get their fill from the natural foods spread around on the floor of their cage. In an emergency when natural foods are not available, softened dog/cat food may be used. Once on natural diet, discontinue the formula.

In the wild, opossums are usually weaned by the 106th day, however it might take you a bit longer. A natural diet should include fruits, grain, eggs, frogs, worms, dead mice, and chicken. Offer a balance of meat and vegetation. If you observe that the opossums are eating one food group exclusively (e.g., fruit), include softened high-protein dog/cat food in the diet to help balance the diet.

RELEASING

When the opossums are fully furred and eating on their own, move them to a larger cage. Begin taking the cage outside and leaving it for several hours. Gradually increase the time outside. When the opossums are weaned and eating a natural diet, they can be moved to a large, permanent outdoor cage. The outside cage should be completely predator-proof. Be sure there are water-proofed areas to allow escape from rain and one or more nesting boxes. Add natural landscaping in the cage that can include such features as logs, rocks, soil area, branches and a water source. Do not put food in a dish-- rather, spread it out in the cage among the natural features. Human contact should be limited to what is necessary to feed the animal, clean the cage, and maintain a fresh water supply.

Once the opossums have been living outside and eating natural foods for at least 10 days, release can be considered. Check the weather forecast before releasing and wait for a predicted period of at least 3 days without rain or dramatic drops in temperature. Also, make sure the opossums are well fed before release. There may be several days when they eat very little and must live off body reserves. Body length, not counting the tail, should be at least 12 inches. Release the opossums in deciduous woodlands with a fresh water source. Do not release near human habitation or roads. Place a food supply at the release site under a wood structure for protection from weather.

SPECIAL NOTES FROM VOLUNTEERS

Opossums make a hissing sound when they are upset or frightened.

Save chicken parts that you don't eat (backs, necks, etc.) to feed to the opossums.

The following additional information is from a volunteer who has had success raising opossums from the hairless embryo age (pouch babies).

The opossum is a marsupial (pouched) rather than a placental mammal. The pouch young require specialized housing. The pouch protects the babies from the external environment, keeps them at or near the body temperature of the mother, and protects them against dehydration. The atmosphere inside the pouch is gaseous with a decreased concentration of oxygen (air breathed in) and an increased concentration of carbon dioxide (air breathed out) that results from the young rebreathing a relatively limited amount of pouch gas. Three known criteria are critical for the environment of the pouch young, listed as follows in descending order of importance: TEMPERATURE 90°-95°F, HUMIDITY/DEHYDRATION, and CARBON DIOXIDE.

HOUSING

Place a heating pad under an aquarium or comparable container, positioning it under a portion of the nest area.

Soak a large cloth in hot water; wring and fold to fit inside the bottom of the container. The bottom should feel warm, not hot, to the touch (young opossums do not always move off an area that is too hot, consequently they can die).

Place the babies in a small pouch-like enclosure. Fold the open ends over, tuck them under the front of the pouch, and place the pouch in the nest area of the container.

> Pouches can be made by sewing 3 sides of a tightly woven fabric--cotton flannel is good (the outside of the flannel becomes the inside of the pouch). The open end can be sewn with velcro to permit closing or a drawstring can be added if

31

the pouch will be hung. Since opossums cling and their toenails can come off easily, rough, loosely woven fabrics such as terry cloth should NOT be used. Pouch size can be 6" X 8" to 8" X 10". NOTE: If there is only one opossum, a small stuffed animal should be placed in the pouch with it.

Cover the top of the container with a wet towel. If humidity of 85%-90% can be achieved without doing this, cover with a dry towel.

Rewet towels as necessary to maintain humidity.

FEEDING FOR HAIRLESS OPOSSUMS

Although opossum neonates readily suck while in the pouch of the mother, they will rarely suck from a bottle, syringe, or eyedropper. For this reason feeding, though possible, is extremely time-consuming and frustrating for the animal and the rehabilitator. It can take up to 2 hours to hand-feed 6 or 7 opossums.

Using a catheter attached to a syringe or a small 1/2 cc syringe, twist the tip of the catheter or syringe gently into the opossum's mouth. Gently press the plunger slowly and release 1/4 to 1/2 cc of formula, pause for 5 seconds and then continue, pausing after each amount is given. Opossums can be fed a maximum of 1 1/2 cc per ounce of body weight per feeding. After the feeding, the stomach should be gently rounded, not taut. Stimulate to eliminate after each feeding.

They require a feeding every 3 hours around the clock.

SPECIAL NOTES

Lightly cover embryos with lanolin or baby oil once or twice a day.

Caution! Small litters composed of pouch young whose eyes are closed, starting to open, or have just opened can be raised together if all are comparable in physical development. Mutilation and cannibalism can result when older juveniles from separate litters are housed together, particularly if the housing unit is small. Release when they are about 12" long. Although they are self-sufficient when smaller, they are more subject to predation.

32

If baby opossums can run around, they can eat on their own.

If the opossums are eating on their own, you need not stimulate them.

The development of a 60-day-old opossum is comparable to that of a placental mammal at birth.

The earliest time that an embryo can be removed from the nipple and reattached is 29 days of age. Between Days 55 and 68 its mouth fully opens. Between Days 58 and 70 the eyes open.

Between Day 97 and Day 104, they normally are weaned.

There are many pitfalls (many we still don't understand) in raising very young opossums, so be prepared to lose some of them.

BATS

The Kalamazoo Nature Center Animal Care Program has not raised any species of bats.

However, in the last several years the Nature Center has received 20-25 Brown Bats and 1 Hoary Bat with 2 young.

All Brown Bats were found in various states of hibernation. In most instances, the bats were put back in an environment which would allow them to continue their hibernation for the balance of the winter. Such environments were protected from the weather and had temperatures of less than 42°F and more than 25-29°F. If possible, the bats were kept from warming up and using valuable fat deposits before being relocated in a suitable environment to continue hibernation.

In 1978, the Nature Center received a female Hoary Bat, which had been stunned by a car; 2 young were clinging to her chest. She was placed in a warm, quiet location in a box until she regained consciousness. However, she seemed unable to fly. In a box containing a stick which formed a perch, the bat learned to hang upside down in a natural position. The young clung to her or crawled off and occasionally hung by themselves. They appeared to be of nursing age.

It was difficult to get the bat to eat; placing raw liver and liver blood in a shallow jar lid and pressing the food and fluid against her nose seemed to get her started. She learned to lick the food off her nose and take bits of liver from a toothpick held against her mouth. Later, the jar lid was placed so that she could feed directly from it on her own while hanging upside down from the perch.

Cottage cheese, plain yogurt, and occasionally wheat germ were added to the raw liver along with a balanced vitamin formula. The bat fed only at night, as is her natural habit. Fresh food was provided nightly.

After approximately 1 week, and several unsuccessful attempts at flight, she gained enough strength and coordination to fly away with her two young.

We have included this experience for reference and use by others who may have bats brought to them that are merely stunned or weak. We do not suggest keeping bats for any length of time beyond what is absolutely necessary for recovery nor do we suggest handling them. They have very sharp teeth, do bite, and are known carriers of rabies. Various references describe them as being difficult to keep in captivity--most seem to die if kept over 3-5 weeks.

RACCOONS

IN THE WILD

Raccoons are among the most widely distributed animals in the world, living in almost all parts of the western hemisphere, Russia, and islands off Alaska. Average body temperature of an adult raccoon ranges from 97°-102°F. In winter, raccoons undergo a period of dormancy which should not be confused with true hibernation. Winter sleep may be broken by periods of warm weather and if food is scarce, raccoons must rely heavily on accumulated body fat to see them through. Up to 60 percent of female raccoons may mate as juveniles although males generally do not breed until the second year.

Mating in northern climates occurs generally in January to March. The Nature Center has received infant raccoons in March and September; however, most orphaned raccoons are received in May and June. Gestation ranges from 60-70 days.

The average litter size is 4-6 young. Eyes and ear canals are closed at birth, but usually open after 18-24 days. At birth, the raccoon is covered with a thin layer of hair. The facial mask hair develops at 2 weeks and the tail rings develop at 3 weeks. At 6 weeks, guard hairs appear and a molt begins at seven weeks. In captivity raccoons have been observed crawling and walking at 4-6 weeks of age. At 7 weeks they can walk and climb and, because of increased mobility, begin exploring outside the den. Wild young raccoons are able to follow the mother and forage at 8-12 weeks of age. Wild raccoons are weaned before the age of 16 weeks and before growing permanent teeth.

By late fall, they may weigh 15 pounds or more (about 50% being body fat stored for winter) and be independent. In some cases, raccoon families may winter together. Favorite shelters include hollow trees and limbs, crevices, caves, abandoned buildings, and ground burrows of foxes or badgers.

Raccoons are omnivorous, eating a wide variety of plants and animals. The most common foods include fleshy fruits (grapes, cherries, berries of all kinds, apples). Raccoons also eat nuts of all kinds, corn, a wide variety of grains, fungi, grasses, crayfish, fishes, insects (beetles, caterpillars), earthworms, rodents, squirrels, birds, eggs, reptiles, and frogs. They forage mostly at night.

It is important to introduce young raccoons to natural smells, sights, foods, and climbing limbs as early as possible so the correct associations are made in the memory cells--this enhances their adjustment to the natural world and better insures their survival upon release.

Raccoons seem to be the cause of more problems for wildlife rehabilitators than many other animals. Raccoons can carry any of three kinds of distemper, rabies, and a number of parasites, including roundworms, as well as bacterial and viral diseases. To protect volunteers and the public from the transmission of parasites and diseases that raccoons can carry, we share a number of our policies and practices.

Avoid raising a raccoon alone if possible. It may imprint upon humans and may not learn coping and social survival behaviors which enable it to be accepted among raccoons in the wild.

Use gloves at all times when handling raccoons. For young raccoons still fed by hand, white plastic surgical gloves work well.

WHAT TO DO FIRST
When you first receive baby raccoons, check the body temperature immediately. A raccoon's temperature is higher than yours so if the animals do not feel warm, you should get the temperature back up to normal immediately. The quickest and most efficient way is by using your own body heat--hold the animals either in your hands or under your shirt. Also, you

can use a heating pad with several layers of towelling separating the body from the heat source; a warm bottle wrapped in a towel is a good substitute.

If the skin tents when it is pinched and the raccoons are weak and listless, the animals are probably dehydrated. After the animals regain normal body temperature, they should be given a small drink of re-hydrating solution every 15 minutes over the next hour. Re-hydrating solution: 1 tsp. salt, 3 tbs. sugar in 1 quart warm water.

Baby raccoons should be checked for ticks--examine the animals all over, including inside the ears and between the toes. If you find ticks, use flea and tick powder (feline) as directed on the container. Also, you can put a cat flea collar in the box under the newspaper. Tick dip solution (available from a veterinarian) is very effective for severe tick infestation. Some tick solutions seem to affect the nervous systems of very young animals adversely (see section on mange for help).

During the first few hours with a volunteer, some baby raccoons spend much of the time crying because they are upset, frightened, and probably hungry.

Do not try to feed them until they calm down a bit. Sometimes holding them cupped in your hands will work and sometimes leaving them in a quiet place for an hour or 2 will help. In any event, the first couple of feedings will be difficult until you get used to each other.

HOUSING

Line any small box with newspaper; then add flannel or towelling. The sides of the box must be high enough so that the baby raccoons can't climb out.

If a heating pad is used, place it outside and under 1/4 to 1/3 of the box and up one side. This allows the animals to select the amount of warmth needed. Start the pad on low heat and use your hand to determine whether the warmth is coming through the box--it should feel warm, not hot.

If a light bulb is used, hang an ordinary 60-watt bulb near the box and position the light over one end of the box so that the temperature will vary from one end to the other. Make sure the animals cannot reach the bulb and be burned.

A hot water bottle wrapped in a towel can be warming and very comforting to baby raccoons, especially if a raccoon must be raised alone.

The size and depth of the box should be adjusted as the raccoons become more mobile. As they get older and begin crawling, they will need a nesting box and a large sturdy cage where they will have room for exercise and will be able to select one specific area for elimination of body wastes. Clean the box at least twice a day--morning and evening. Some volunteers line the box or cage with a portion of shower curtain and then place newspaper over it, thus keeping the box from being ruined with moisture. Until ready to place them outside in a large cage (when they no longer need extra heat), some volunteers use a bathtub to hold them--it's easy to clean and the animal can't get out. If a tub is used, put a nesting box in it.

To be consistent with our philosophy that wild animals should be exposed as early as possible to the natural smells, texture, and associations with the natural environment, be certain to have logs, soil, and rocks in the cage or box when the raccoons begin to walk and climb actively.

Because raccoons can carry roundworms (as well as other worms), and because roundworms can be fatal to humans (especially children, if the eggs or worms are ingested), Rehabilitation Program volunteers are taught always to wear gloves when cleaning raccoon boxes and cages and to burn all wastes and papers containing waste. Other than destroying the feces with a blow-torch, this is the only safe way to kill the eggs and worms of roundworms and to insure the health and safety of volunteers and their families.

See **POLICIES FOR THE PROTECTION OF PEOPLE** at the end of this chapter.

FEEDING
Use lightweight surgical gloves when handling baby raccoons. Use powdered formula (Esbilac or Unilact) and mix according to directions, usually 1 part milk to 3 parts very warm water. Water can be very warm when mixing so it will feel just warm to the inside of your wrist when you are ready to feed.

Add 3-4 drops of a balanced vitamin per cup of formula. If the raccoons are fed properly and slowly at first, there should be no formula sucked into the lungs (this may cause pneumonia). However, if the formula needs to be thickened to prevent aspirating (breathing food), use baby cereal. If the raccoons are not taking the formula well, a small amount of Karo syrup or honey may help, but discontinue the use of sweeteners after 2 days to prevent stomach upset. Feed formula warmed.

Raccoons may be fed with a variety of utensils including an eyedropper, syringe, or pet-nurser bottle. A number of volunteers prefer to use only syringes because they feel they have more control over getting formula into the baby's mouth this way. They also feel that syringes do not encourage the strong sucking behavior that is generated by nursing bottles, thus making it much easier for the young to be weaned. Other volunteers prefer the eyedropper or pet-nurser, feeling that there should be some sucking satisfaction for the raccoons, and they can cope with weaning difficulties.

Healthy raccoons need to be fed every 3-4 hours, depending on how well they are doing. It may take 1-2 days and several tries before the raccoons become accustomed to a new feeding object in their mouths and new-tasting food. Placing the syringe or eyedropper in the mouth and squeezing a small amount of formula on the back of the tongue helps to get reluctant raccoons to feed. Be careful not to overfeed raccoons; they often keep sucking even when their stomachs are full. The stomach should be rounded but not tight. Continued unnecessary sucking may become a habit and will make weaning more difficult. Stimulate the young to eliminate wastes after each feeding by rubbing the belly and genital areas with a warm damp cloth.

Discontinue the stimulation after a minute or 2 whether they have eliminated or not. Do this after each feeding until the eyes are fully opened, or until you observe evidence in the box that the raccoons are able to eliminate on their own. Often the raccoon bowel movement will be runny and yellowish until it begins eating solid food. A weak raccoon will need to be fed more often than every 3-4 hours. Depending on its condition, it is recommended that a weak raccoon be fed every 2 hours or whatever appears necessary to keep increasing the animal's strength.

When raccoons have their eyes open and begin to get teeth (3-4 weeks old), gradually begin adding strained baby food (meat, fruit, and vegetables), applesauce, yogurt, and/or natural foods to the formula. In the wild, raccoons are often weaned by the age of 6-8 weeks. This should be the goal for all raccoons being prepared for release.

There are two schools of thought on proper weaning; both are listed.

Method A

Pour formula or yogurt (one with wild fruit) into a shallow dish once a day at first. Dip the raccoons' faces into the food in the dish. At first they will not like it, but soon will learn to lick it off their faces and then from the dish. As you observe that the raccoons have learned to feed themselves more independently and fill their stomachs, substitute one of the independent feedings for a feeding with a syringe or bottle. This gradual substitution should take place over 2-3 days. It is important to make certain that the raccoons are getting their fill at each feeding. It is also important to leave food in the larger housing box so the animals may be self-feeding when they become hungry. At 6-7 weeks, raccoons should be fairly independent of the bottle. As teeth appear, pour formula or yogurt over softened puppy chow or a balanced, softened, dry cat or dog food. Encourage gumming and eating of the heavier food. As the animals fully develop teeth, they will eat plain dry cat or dog food--these are temporary balanced diets. Begin leaving natural foods in the box or cage--raw (boned) fish, wild berries, soft buds, etc. Although dry dog or cat food will serve as a staple food while raccoons are in your care, every effort should be made to introduce their natural food into their diet.

Raccoons are very messy eaters. It is wise to have a separate box for feeding during the early weaning stages so they do not track food all over their bedding. They may need to be cleaned off lightly after each self-feeding. Do not let them chill. As they master self-feeding, food and water dishes should be left in the box so they can feed on their own.

Method B

This alternate method resembles more directly what occurs in the wild at weaning time for young raccoons. Eliminate the intermediate stage of pouring

41

formula or yogurt over dry cat or dog food in a dish. In the wild, raccoons are not likely to be eating from dishes nor are they likely to find yogurt and soft dry cat or dog food. Introducing them to these smells and tastes at such an impressionable early stage in their learning may make it more difficult to unlearn these associations later. At the age of 5-6 weeks, or when the raccoons become mobile, leave soft natural foods in the cage (examples include raw/boned fish, wild berries, and other things young raccoons might put into their mouths on their first exploratory trips with the mother). Place some of these foods in the mouths of the animals (use gloves) on a daily basis, being patient because it will take several tries before they learn to chew and swallow food with bulk in it. Feed formula to the raccoons on a regular schedule throughout this period (in the wild the young raccoons will nurse from the mother until they can chew and swallow whole foods). When the raccoons are able to chew and swallow whole food, reduce the number of formula feedings gradually over a period of several days. This will allow the raccoons to become hungry enough to begin to feed themselves from the food in their box or cage. Be certain to provide enough natural food and be certain that the animals are getting enough to eat. After the raccoons have developed teeth and have begun to feed themselves independently, add dry cat or dog food to the foods in the box or cage to provide a basic balanced diet with the proper vitamins for growth. Continue to use dry cat or dog food only as a base; emphasize water and natural foods.

RELEASING

When raccoons develop sufficient motor coordination, are fully furred, and are eating natural foods, place them in a cage for exercise and sunshine. They soon explore and begin foraging for insects, roots, etc. By this time the cage--the bigger the better--should be outdoors. Michigan law requires a minimum 6' x 6' x 6' cage **for 1 raccoon**. The Nature Center encourages building the biggest cage possible beyond the minimum. The best materials to use are hardware cloth and wood. The cage can then be used for other species, including squirrels and songbirds, without fear of escape. Cages should be wired on the bottom and top as well as sides and have one side (usually the west or north side) and the top covered with wood or a tarpaulin against the weather. Because raccoons move horizontally and vertically, the cage should include tree limbs and stumps (for climbing or housing), fresh water, and 1 or more water-proofed nest boxes high in the cage.

From this point on, a balanced diet of natural foods (see list in **In The Wild** section of this chapter) should be provided, with dry dog or cat food used as a staple. Raccoons should also have been vaccinated against distemper and, if old enough, against rabies, been wormed several times (see vaccination and worming schedules at the end of this account), and been weaned emotionally from the caretaker. The Nature Center has used two methods for releasing the animals into the wild.

The method currently being utilized and taught to volunteers is to have each individual volunteer handle the release of the raccoons he/she has raised. The risk of disease contamination among raccoons is less with this method. However, raccoons prepared for release in groups learn coping and social survival behaviors which they might not learn otherwise. Each volunteer prepares the animals and selects a release site which meets the Rehabilitation Program release guidelines.

Another method of releasing raccoons began on Nature Center property. After the raccoons were prepared for release by the volunteers in their homes, the animals were put into a large release pen with up to 30 other raccoons. They stayed in this enclosure for about 3 weeks before they were taken to an appropriate release area. This method allowed them to "socialize" with other raccoons and to learn to establish a "pecking order." Human contact was kept to a minimum. However, the Nature Center discontinued this method of release because the large raccoon population in the small area appeared to concentrate pathogens and outbreaks of diseases occurred.

RELEASE CRITERIA

Release sites must be selected with the following criteria in mind: water (stream, lake, marsh, swamp, etc.) must be on the site; a woods with logs for climbing and nesting must be on the site; ideally, the site should be a minimum of 2-3 miles from the nearest road or human habitation. Sites may be on private or public land.

The raccoons should be wild. They should not be tame enough to walk up to or follow any human and should be fearful of people. They should be difficult to catch. The Rehabilitation Program has developed guidelines for catching raccoons for release without jeopardizing the volunteer who must catch them. Heavy welder's gloves and a strong net should be used. When the raccoon is netted, it will struggle and scream. Firmly take hold of the fur at the back of the neck in a manner that the raccoon cannot turn its head and bite, then lift the animal into the nearby cage for transport to the release area. Another method of holding a properly raised wild raccoon is to pin its head to the ground once it is in the net, then place your hands around the body at the shoulders with the forelegs between your index and third fingers. Make certain your thumbs firmly holding the head to keep it from turning to bite.

RELEASE PROCEDURE

Check the weather forecast before releasing raccoons and wait for a predicted period of at least 3 days without rain or dramatic drops in temperature.

Once the release site is reached, the animals should be transported into the property, as far as possible from roads. Depending on the number of raccoons to be released, 25-50 pounds of dry dog food should be brought, plus a wood A-frame shelter to place over the dry food to protect it from rain and from turning to mush before the raccoons can find food on their own in their new territory. Place the dry dog food at the base of a tree with the open-ended A-frame shelter over it. Place the release cage against the tree and open the door. Try to see to it that the raccoons climb the tree near the dog food. They will find their way down after the humans have left, and find the food supply which will help sustain them until they become fully acclimated to their new home. Some raccoons will wander about the area near the food or explore in the nearby water. Leave the release area immediately--do not stay with the raccoons. If you stay in the area, you risk the chance that, when they tire of exploring, they will find you and follow you back to the car. In this case, you will have to go through the whole procedure again, with greater difficulty.

Ideally, raccoons should be released no later than the second or third week in August to allow adequate time to establish a territory and put on a fat layer (to help survive partial hibernation) before winter. Late raccoons (those born in late May, June, or July) may either be held over until spring or released in September or early October near a food supply that is replenished once before winter.

TIPS FROM VOLUNTEERS

If you have difficulty making the raccoons release their claws, hold them by the back of the neck.

Scratching the back of a raccoon's neck often stimulates a sucking response.

If raccoons get up a tree and won't come down, spray the animals lightly with a garden hose. They will usually be disturbed enough by the water to overcome their fear and begin to back down the tree.

If raccoons get bloated, cut back on the amount of formula considerably until the problem straightens out. Substitute re-hydration formula for some feedings. Also, submerge the lower body (below the "waist") in warm water and massage it for about five minutes. The bloat should disappear in a couple of hours.

Raccoons seem to need more attention--holding and touching--in their first 6 weeks if they are being raised alone. Single raccoons are harder to raise than 2 or more at a time. Every effort should be made to see that they are not raised alone because they tend to imprint more easily on humans and do not go wild without difficulty.

Raccoons resist being weaned even when they are old enough to be eating on their own. **BE FIRM!**

POLICIES FOR THE PROTECTION OF PEOPLE

BITES

Any raccoon that bites a volunteer is euthanized. The head is sent to the nearest public or animal health institution to be tested for rabies, for the protection of rehabilitation volunteers and anyone else who had contact with the raccoon.

GLOVES

All volunteers are taught to wear gloves at all times when handling raccoons to protect themselves from possible disease or parasite transfer, and to guard against bites. It is heartbreaking for volunteers and their families who have spent hours raising raccoons to be bitten by a raccoon as a result of carelessness and then have to have the animal they cared for euthanized. Light surgical gloves are recommended and provided by the Program when raccoons are young. Heavy welder's gloves or bird of prey gloves are recommended for handling and cleaning cages when raccoons are older.

All volunteers are taught to wash their hands after any handling of raccoons or caging materials.

VACCINATIONS

All raccoons in the Rehabilitation Program are vaccinated against distemper and rabies and are given regular wormings.

Age 5-6 weeks:	1st distemper shot
	1st worming
3-week intervals:	each subsequent worming
Age 8-10 weeks:	2nd distemper shot
	rabies shot

Vaccinations are administered by veterinarians and rehabilitation staff. NO vaccines are sent home with volunteers. Volunteers are responsible for picking up their worming medicines from the office on schedule. The office keeps detailed records of due dates for vaccinations and worming. Before releasing raccoons, experienced rehabilitation staff, under the authorization of the veterinarian, visit the homes of volunteers to administer the final vaccinations to raccoons that are too wild to transport.

Volunteers are required to obtain a tetanus shot. The Program pays for the staff's pre-immunization rabies shots through the Kalamazoo County Health Department. Through the Michigan Department of Public Health, pre-immunization vaccinations have been provided for groups of 20 or more with a procedure for up-to-date titer checks.

46

BADGERS

IN THE WILD

Baby badgers are born in May or June and usually number from 1-5 per litter. Born blind, the kits open their eyes at 4 weeks and are weaned at 8 weeks. The mother carries food to her offspring until they are 3/4 grown. Adult badgers are about 2 feet long from the tip of the nose to the end of the tail. They weigh 12-20 pounds. The badgers' diet is almost exclusively meat. They prey on ground squirrels, moles, woodchucks, rabbits, snakes, and field mice. Badgers make their dens underground in upland grasslands. They do most of their hunting at night.

WHAT TO DO FIRST

When you first receive baby badgers, be sure the animals are warm to the touch. If they feel cold or if they don't have their eyes open yet, put them on a heating pad. Separate the young from the heating pad with several layers of towelling material and warm them slowly.

Check to be sure the animals are not dehydrated. To check for this, look for listlessness and/or gently pinch the animal's skin. If the skin "tents" (stays up rather than going back to a normal position), begin giving the animals small amounts (a dropper-full at first) of re-hydration solution: 1 tsp. salt, 3 tbs. sugar in 1 quart warm water.

When the badgers are warm and hydrated, begin the feeding schedule.

HOUSING

Line a box with newspapers and soft materials.

If a heating pad is used, place it outside and under half of the box. Start the pad on low and check to be sure it is warm enough inside the box. If a light is chosen as the heat source, hang a 60-watt bulb over the box at 1 end. Be sure the bulb is out of reach of the animals but is near enough to provide the badgers with proper heat.

FEEDING

Mix 1 part powdered Esbilac or Unilact formula to 3 parts warm water plus 3-4 drops balanced liquid pet vitamins. Thicken the formula with baby rice cereal. The badgers can be fed with a baby bottle because they have large mouths even at a young age.

Feed every 4 hours. Feed the badgers until their stomachs are full and rounded--but never tight. Stimulate the young after each feeding by rubbing the belly and genital areas with a warm, damp cloth until the animals have eliminated. Discontinue this stimulation after a minute or so whether the animals have eliminated or not. Do this after each feeding until the eyes are fully opened or the animals are eliminating on their own.

When the badgers are 4-5 weeks old, start adding egg yolk to the formula. When they are about 6-8 weeks old, start giving them small pieces of liver or beef heart in a dish with their formula. Dip their noses in the dish to get them started licking. Over a period of several days reduce the amount of formula and put dry cat food or puppy chow plus a bowl of water in their cage. Also put in raw beef, liver, or fresh pieces of mice. Badgers are weaned quite easily.

Feed weaned badgers at night. Do not use dishes for food, but place food on soil on the bottom of the cage to teach natural food-finding habits.

RELEASING

When the badgers are eating on their own, put them in a well-built outdoor cage with a strong wire bottom on it. Place food and water in the cage. Place a shelter box in the cage also, with a soil pile for digging. If badgers are let out to exercise, watch them carefully because when they start digging they will dig out of sight very quickly.

When they are eating mostly natural foods, are three-quarters grown, and have had success in catching live prey, they are ready to begin the release process. Release in dry upland areas near woods and water. Place food (dry dog food or beef or mice) under a wood A-frame at the release site and leave the area at once. Check the weather forecast before releasing and wait for a predicted period of at least 3 days without rain or dramatic drops in temperature. Release away from people, farms, and dogs.

TIPS FROM ANIMAL CARE VOLUNTEERS
Baby badgers will growl and snarl even before their eyes have opened if they are scared or hungry.

Badgers are fearless--unafraid of anything even at a very young age.

Badgers are a protected animal in Michigan and in most other states.

SKUNKS

IN THE WILD
Breeding usually takes place in February or March and the 2-10 young are born in early May. The newborn's eyes and ears are closed and it has only a thin, short coat of fine hair which already exhibits the striped pattern of the adults. Skunks become fully furred at 2 weeks, their eyes open at 17-28 days, and they are weaned at about 2 months.

Truly omnivorous, skunks eat more insects than most carnivores. Small mammals and birds (including poultry), eggs, and vegetable matter make up about half of their diet; invertebrates, including insects and their larvae and pupae, account for the remainder.

With the approach of cold December weather, skunks retreat to a deep underground den where they become dormant. A mother and her young may remain inactive for long periods, whereas the males tend to be more active during mild periods throughout the winter. By late February, skunks begin to appear more frequently and by the end of March full activity is resumed.

Skunks have a wide tolerance in their habitat requirements, but seem to prefer semi-open areas of mixed forests and grassland.

Michigan Department of Natural Resources regulations prohibit Nature Center volunteers from raising skunks because of their reportedly high incidence of rabies. Check your state's regulations before handling skunks.

WHAT TO DO FIRST

If the baby skunks you receive don't feel warm, warm them up slowly--holding them in your hands is an effective way to begin getting their temperature back to normal. The babies should feel warm to you because a skunk's normal temperature is higher than yours. You can also warm them by using a warm hot water bottle or a heating pad on warm or low with several layers of towelling separating the babies from the heat source.

After the babies are sufficiently warmed, the next concern is whether they are dehydrated. If the animals appear weak and listless and if the skin tents when it is pinched, the animals may be dehydrated. After the skunks regain their normal body temperature, they should be given a small drink (1 or 2 eyedroppers-full) of re-hydrating solution every 15 minutes over the next hour: 1 tsp. salt, 3 tbs. sugar in 1 quart warm water.

Next check the babies for ticks, lice, etc. If you find any, use cat flea powder.

If you are sure the young are warm, hydrated, and de-liced, proceed to prepare housing and to begin a normal feeding schedule.

HOUSING

Housing for baby skunks is the same as for raccoons, squirrels, and other medium-sized mammals.

Line any small box with newspaper and towelling. The sides of the box must be high enough so that the skunks can't climb out. Place a heating pad outside and under 1/4 to 1/3 of the box and up one side. This allows needed warmth but also allows the animals to get away from the heat. Start the pad on low and use your hand to feel the warmth coming through the box--the box should feel warm, never hot.

As skunks get older and more mobile, adjust the size and depth of the box.

As the skunks become furred, open their eyes, and walk, begin preparing them for life outside. During warm days, take the skunks outside and gradually acclimate them to staying outside all day and night. When outdoors permanently, the cage should be big enough for the animals to exercise, contain a small nesting box, and have an area protected from wind and rain. Put old logs and piles of fresh soil in the skunks' cage regularly so the animals can get used to digging--this is how most of the food will be found once they are released.

FEEDING

Use 1 part powdered formula (Esbilac or Unilact) to 3 parts warm water. Add 3 drops pet vitamins per cup of formula. The warmed formula can be fed to the skunks using an eyedropper, a syringe, or a pet- or doll-nursing bottle.

Before beginning to feed the skunks, be sure they are fully awake. Gently massage the infants until they appear fully awake. Sometimes the massage will stimulate a sucking reflex.

If the skunks are healthy and eating well, feed them every 4 hours. If the animals are weak or not eating well, they will have to be fed more often until they regain their strength and begin to eat vigorously.

Usually the skunks will stop sucking when full. The stomach should feel rounded and firm--but never tight or bloated. It is just as unhealthy to overfeed young as it is to underfeed them.

Following each feeding, rub each infant's belly and genital area with a warm, damp cloth. This usually stimulates the infants to urinate or have a bowel movement; but don't worry if it doesn't work every time. Discontinue the stimulation after a minute whether or not they have eliminated. This activity can be discontinued altogether once the animals begin to eliminate on their own without stimulation. You'll know this has occurred when you see droppings and urine in the box. Each infant should be independent of the stimulation by the time its eyes have opened.

When the skunks' eyes have opened (sometime between the 17th and 21st days), begin offering them a natural diet. Skunks are omnivorous and can eat a wide variety of food. A natural diet can include the following: insects such as grasshoppers, crickets, beetles, and bees; spiders; earthworms; snails;

clams; crayfish; frogs; eggs; and minnows. They also eat field mice and other small rodents. They eat numerous species of berries including blackberry, black cherry, blueberries, raspberries; also grasses, nuts, roots, grains, corn, and other vegetation. (In an emergency, when natural food is not available, the skunks can be offered softened, high-protein dog food as a temporary substitute for the natural diet.)

The skunks will begin showing an interest in the natural diet when they are about 2 months old. Continue offering them the formula every 4-6 hours until they are able to get their fill from the natural foods you have spread around on the floor of the cage. If you observe that the skunks are eating a food group exclusively (e.g., fruit), you may include softened, high-protein dog food in the diet to help maintain a balance.

RELEASING

When the skunks are beginning to eat a natural diet, move them to a larger cage. Begin leaving them in the cage outside for several hours a day. Leave the cage in a partly sunny/partly shady area that is away from human activity. Gradually increase the time outside.

When the skunks are weaned and eating a natural diet, they can be moved to a large, permanent, completely predator-proof, outdoor cage. Be sure that there are water-proofed areas to allow escape from rain. In the cage add a small nesting box and natural landscaping, such as logs, rocks, soil areas, branches, and a water source. Do not put the food in a dish--but spread it in the cage among the natural features. Human contact should be limited to what is necessary to feed the animals, clean the cage (remove droppings plus any uneaten food daily), and maintain a fresh water supply.

Once the skunks have been living outside and eating natural foods for at least 10 days, release can be considered. Check the weather forecast before releasing and wait for a predicted period of at least 3 days without rain or dramatic drops in temperature. Make sure the animals are well fed before they are released--there may be several days when they eat very little and may have to live off body reserves.

Skunks have a wide tolerance in their habitat requirements, but seem to prefer semi-open areas of mixed forests and grassland. Do not release near human habitation. Place several days' worth of food near the release site.

SPECIAL NOTES

Skunks seem to be able to spray from a very early age. Most skunks, however, will not spray unless truly alarmed or threatened. Skunks issue a warning before spraying--they will stamp the feet and turn the tail toward the target. Baby skunks acquire a musky scent at about 6-8 weeks of age, an added incentive to getting them into outside cages. If startled or introduced to a new experience, skunks will point the "sprayer" but will not spray until they stamp the feet first.

Skunks are listed as high-incidence carriers of rabies, and many states prohibit anyone's possessing a skunk for any reason. At the time of writing this manual, area veterinarians are cautious about giving rabies vaccinations of any kind because government data indicate a lack of research on the effects on wild animals. If an animal appears abnormal or ill to you, call a supervisor to verify symptoms; a veterinarian should be contacted.

If rabies vaccination is given, make certain it is a killed vaccine.

If your state laws or rules prohibit the possession of skunks, and you do not wish to dispose of the animals, the Center has found the following suggestion helpful. Young skunks that have opened their eyes and can walk can be taken to a natural area and released into a brush pile or downed log. Soft food should be placed next to the log or brush pile where the skunks were released. Because young skunks learn to feed themselves very early, they will partake of the food placed there for them and have some chance at survival. The food supply may be replenished 2-3 times a week and eventually discontinued after the skunks are old enough to fend for themselves. By using the above suggestion, apparently you are not breaking the law; you have given the skunks some opportunity to survive; and you do not handle or touch them, thus not exposing yourself to possible disease.

FOXES

(Red, Gray)

IN THE WILD

The Nature Center has raised both Gray and Red Foxes. It is believed that the Red Fox was introduced into North America from Europe and that the Gray Fox was native to the eastern United States.

Foxes breed primarily from mid-January to mid-March, generally mating for life. The dens are usually underground for Red Foxes and in wood or brush piles, rocks, or hollow trees for Gray Foxes. Gray Fox pups are mostly hairless at birth and have dark skin. Red Fox pups at birth have gray, silky fur which changes to yellowish brown before becoming the color of the adult.

At about 14 weeks, guard hairs appear on the legs and the coat becomes a reddish brown. Red Foxes open their eyes at 8-9 days while Gray Fox pups open their eyes at 10-12 days. Red Fox pups begin to walk at about 3 weeks and their ears become erect at about 4 weeks of age. The average litter for Red Foxes is between 4-7 young, but the average litter for Gray Foxes is 3-4 young.

Fox pups remain in the den for the first month of life and then, at about 10 weeks of age, they explore the immediate area around the den. At 12-14 weeks, they roam various sections of the parents' home territory and disperse to live on their own in September-October. Males usually leave home before females.

The most important criteria in selection of habitat by foxes appears to be ground cover, followed by abundance of food, competition by others of the same species or other species, diversity of habitat and occurrence of natural barriers such as rivers or lakes. Although both species prefer a diversity of habitat, the Red Fox prefers rolling farmland, open croplands, pastures, mixed hardwood trees, and field edges. The Gray Fox prefers the deeper woodlands, although it also uses the fields and forest edges. Foxes like to climb trees occasionally or sit on high moraines looking over large areas for food and watching for predators (humans and dogs).

The food of foxes ranges from fruits and insects to small mammals and birds. Often foxes will cache their food for later feeding during lean times. The main food for the Red Fox is the Meadow Mouse while the main food for the Gray Fox is the Cottontail Rabbit. In the summer, both species consume large quantities of fruits (pears, apples, grapes), insects, corn, wheat, grasses, sedges, and nuts.

The major causes of mortality for foxes are hunting, trapping, and road kills. This should be considered in any release program for foxes. Foxes may carry a number of parasites, as well as distemper and rabies. Foxes at the Nature Center are vaccinated and wormed on a regular basis. Please see the end of this section for the schedule. Gloves are utilized in handling of foxes to prevent any possibility of bites. Should a fox bite someone in the program, the animal would be euthanized and the head sent to the state for rabies diagnosis per the Nature Center's policy.

WHAT TO DO FIRST
When you receive baby foxes, the animals' temperatures are immediately important. A fox's normal temperature is higher than yours so if the animals do not feel warm, you should slowly raise the temperature. The most effective way is by using your own body heat--hold the animals either in your hands or under your shirt. You also can use a warm heating pad with a layer of towelling or newspaper separating the young from the heat source; you can use a hot water bottle wrapped in a towel.

If the skin tents (stays up) when it is pinched and the animals are listless and weak, they are probably dehydrated. After the animals regain normal body temperature, they should be given a small drink of re-hydrating solution every 15 minutes over the next hour: 1 tsp. salt, 3 tbs. sugar in 1 quart warm water. Use an eyedropper or syringe and be careful not to get the solution into the lungs. If the foxes do not begin to respond or to show signs of more energy, continue re-hydration solution for the next 3-4 hours or until the animals begin to show an increase in activity and energy. The use of Nutrical, a high-energy balanced vitamin paste, along with the re-hydration solution will help bring animals back to health.

Baby foxes should be checked for ticks--examine the animal all over including the insides of the ears and between the toes. If you find ticks, use flea and tick powder (feline) as directed on the container. You can also put a cat flea collar in the box under the newspaper. Tick-dip solution (available from a veterinarian) can be very effective for severe infestations; however it may be toxic to the baby fox's nervous sytem and cause convulsions. A solution of lime sulfate is recommended for very young animals. (Consult your supervisor.) Use caution and do not get it into the fox's eyes or nose. Warm immediately and do not chill.

HOUSING

Try to set up housing at all ages for foxes based on their natural needs. See the natural history section. For very young foxes, line any small box with newspaper and then add flannel or towelling. The sides of the box must be high enough so the baby foxes cannot climb out. Because young foxes spend the first month in the den, a dark den-like "house" or enclosure should cover the major part of the box to provide the feeling of underground darkness and security.

For heat there are two possible methods.

Method A

If a heating pad is used, place the pad outside and under 1/4 to 1/3 of the box and up one side of the box. This allows warmth when needed but escape if it is too warm. Start the pad on low heat and use your hand to feel the warmth coming through the box--it should feel warm, not hot. The temperature for the very young foxes should be about 90°F.

Method B
If a light bulb is used, hang an ordinary 60-watt bulb near the box and position the light over one end of the box so that the temperature will vary from one end to the other. Make sure the animals cannot reach the bulb and be burned. Light bulbs do not work as well as heating pads or hot water bottles for mammals.

As the foxes' eyes open and they begin walking, provide a large wire cage and a nest box with towels, rags, or straw for bedding. Remember to refer to the natural history section on the fox for the timing of when the animals begin to walk and explore in the wild. The bottom of the cage may be covered with newspapers and these should be changed once or twice per day, depending on the need. Placing fresh soil and sand in the cage will help the fox associate the natural smells of these earth elements with housing and denning in the wild. As the foxes become furred, discontinue heat and begin placing them outside on warm days. At 6-7 weeks of age, they should be outside on all but the coldest nights. If there is more than 1 fox in the litter, all can be left outside permanently as they will keep each other warm. Foxes require a very large outdoor cage for movement and exercise. The floor should be earth or sand and be kept clean. There should be hollow logs, rock piles, and den boxes with natural bedding. Part of the cage should be sheltered from the weather and there should be logs for climbing and fresh water to drink. The outdoor cage should be located in a private, quiet location away from people and dogs. If possible, the cage should be located on the site where the foxes are to be released so they may return to the cage for food.

FEEDING
Use Esbilac or Unilact and mix 1 part powder to 3 parts warm water. Add 3-4 drops of balanced liquid vitamins and feed with an eyedropper, syringe, or pet-nurser bottle. Foxes 1-2 weeks old may be fed with a regular baby bottle with an enlarged hole. Feedings should be about 4 hours apart for a healthy fox, 2-3 hours apart for a weak fox. Hold the foxes in their natural standing position. If they do not take the bottle easily, gently force open

the mouth and squirt formula onto the tongue, allowing them to swallow. You may have to work a little to get young foxes to learn to suck. Stimulate the young foxes after each feeding by rubbing the belly and genital areas with a warm damp cloth until the animals have had a bowel movement and have urinated. Discontinue after about a minute whether or not the foxes have eliminated. Do this after each feeding until the eyes are fully opened.

After the eyes open (see **IN THE WILD** section of this chapter) and teeth begin to appear, start the process of weaning. There are two approaches to weaning all young foxes.

Method A
Try to follow what would happen in the wild in weaning the young foxes. Provide fresh, raw meat in very little chunks for the young foxes to begin to chew or "mouth." As you observe that they are eating more and more of the meat, eliminate 1 bottle feeding every 3 days or so until the foxes no longer are drinking from the bottle. Fresh water should be provided at all times in the box or cage after the foxes begin to eat meat. Remember to look at what the fox eats in the wild and feed mice, fresh rabbit, some fruit and insects, etc. Foxes raised in our program prefer mice over most other foods. It is important that foxes have the bones and hair for proper digestion. This method of weaning avoids the association of food with dishes and does not build up the expectation or habit of looking for food in dishes. However, foxes will need formula longer than they do in the wild--until they are completely able to sustain themselves on meat and water.

Method B
Pour formula over dry cat food or puppy chow; dip the animals' noses into it. Foxes will lick the formula off their faces and soon learn to pick from the dish and chew the food. Substitute 1 self-feeding session (with a food dish) for 1 bottle feeding per day over a period of about a week. Make certain the foxes are getting a full meal from each "lapping" feeding. The abdomen should look full and round but not tight. Also, begin adding to the food dish pieces of raw meat, including liver. Small mice (cut up or whole) are an excellent food source. At the end of the sixth week foxes should be feeding on their own from the dish. Leave a small pan of water with the food dish in the cage.

RELEASE

As the foxes become fully furred, have teeth, and are feeding on their own, place them outside in a cage large enough (at least 10' long X 4' high) for adequate exercise. The animals should have shelter from the weather and large logs or rocks to sit on. Remember that foxes like dark holes which approximate dens and security. Feed as much natural food as possible--most foxes prefer not to eat dry dog or cat food if they have an adequate daily supply of natural food. If the release pen is not located in the area in which the foxes will be released (to return to it for food), the foxes should be taken for walks on a very long lead so they may learn to hunt and forage. Or live mice, rabbits, or birds should be introduced into the pen so the foxes can learn to hunt and kill their own food before release. Foxes become amazingly adept and quick at learning to catch rodents and grasshoppers if given the opportunity.

When the foxes are fully grown (3-4 months) and have been observed hunting live food consistently, they may be released. Leave the cage door open and continue placing food at the cage site until the animals do not return for 2 weeks. Foxes usually become independent in 2-4 weeks after release. They may do well in the wild for the first week, then return for food in the third week, and then do well in the week following. So, do not assume that the foxes are doing well just because they have not been observed returning to the pen during the first week. It is far better to err on the safe side and put out too much food than to quit too early and have a hungry fox return to find no food at all. Do not release foxes near humans, roads, dogs, or hunting or trapping areas.

SPECIAL NOTES

Foxes raised through the Nature Center's Rehabilitation Program are released from pens on Nature Center property. All are vaccinated for distemper and rabies with a killed rabies vaccine before release. Foxes should never be vaccinated with live rabies vaccine because research has shown that this type of vaccine may actually cause rabies in wild animals. The first distemper vaccination should be given at about 6 weeks of age and the second should be given at 8 weeks of age. At the time of the second distemper shot, the rabies shot is also given. Worming takes place every 3 weeks with the first

60

worming medicine given at 5-6 weeks of age if the animals are healthy. Foxes showing any symptom of disease or broken bones should be treated by a veterinarian.

Some foxes have arrived at the Nature Center stunned or simply weak. These have been re-vitalized through feeding and rest, vaccinated, and released. On one occasion (fall, 1979) a young female fox (vixen) was brought in blinded (age 7-8 weeks). Observation and examination indicated that the principal cause of blindness seemed to be malnutrition. We were unable to determine how long the blindness had existed. After rest, food, and large doses of balanced vitamins, she regained her sight and was released 6 months later in the spring. Occasionally a fox is kept for one full year before release, especially if it has been injured or is unusually weak, to insure adequate maturity and health for survival.

On one occasion, the Rehabilitation Program received a Gray Fox kit and a Red Fox kit in the spring. They were raised together and released from the same pen. Each seemed to accept the other and very little competition was observed between the two species.

WOODCHUCKS

IN THE WILD

The 2-6 small kits per litter are blind and naked at birth but grow quite rapidly. Newborn woodchucks are about 4 1/2" long and weigh 1 ounce. Adults are 16-24" long and weigh 4-12 pounds. By the end of the first month, the young have doubled their length and increased their weight by 5-6 times. They are weaned at about 5-6 weeks of age (June-July) and turn to vegetation for their entire diet, reaching about 2 pounds at 2 months of age. The habitat includes fields, pastures, fence rows, woodlots, and semi-open forests. Their diet consists entirely of green vegetation, including clover, alfalfa, and other wild and cultivated plants. Their home is a burrow in the ground, where they hibernate through the winter.

WHAT TO DO FIRST

When you receive young woodchucks, check each animal's temperature immediately--a woodchuck's normal temperature is higher than yours, so if an animal does not feel warm, you should get the temperature back to normal slowly. The most efficient way is by using your own body heat--either hold the animal in your hands or under your shirt. You also can use a heating pad or hot water bottle wrapped in towelling.

If the baby woodchuck's skin tents when it is pinched, it is probably dehydrated. After the woodchuck regains its normal body temperature, it should be given a small drink (a few drops if the animal is newborn) of re-hydrating solution every 15 minutes for the next hour: 1 tsp. salt, 3 tbs. sugar in 1 quart warm water.

After you are sure the babies are warm and hydrated, prepare housing and begin a normal feeding schedule.

HOUSING

The newborns should be kept in a small box lined with newspapers and soft bedding; heat should be provided.

If a heating pad is used, place the pad outside and under 1/4 to 1/3 of the box and up one side. This allows warmth when needed but escape if it is too warm. Start the pad on low heat and use your hand to feel the warmth coming through the box--it should feel warm, not hot. The temperature for the very young woodchuck should be about 90°F.

If a light bulb is used, hang an ordinary 60-watt (or less) bulb near the box and position the light over one end of the box so that the temperature will vary from one end to the other. Make sure the animal cannot reach the bulb and be burned.

The heat can be removed when the woodchucks are fully furred and seem to be spending most of their time away from the heat.

Enlarge the box (depth and width) as the animals grow and change the bedding and clean the box thoroughly each day. As woodchucks mature, place dirt, fresh grasses, and clover in the box to give the animals early association with the natural smells of the outdoor world.

As soon as the animals are weaned, they should be caged outdoors. The large cage should include a small nesting box and the cage site should allow for both sun and shade at all times plus an area protected from rain.

FEEDING

A woodchuck has a very strong suck and will aspirate ("breathe") its formula unless it is thickened with baby cereal. Mix 1 part Esbilac or Unilact to 3 parts warm water and then add enough baby cereal to thicken the formula slightly. If the woodchucks appear to be newborn, add 1/2 tsp. of steamed bone meal per day until the eyes open. Young animals prefer the formula warmed.

Before beginning to feed the woodchucks, be sure they are fully awake. Sometimes it is helpful to gently massage the animals until they appear fully awake and alert. This massaging action may stimulate a sucking reflex.

Feed the woodchucks with an eyedropper, syringe, or pet-nurser approximately every 4 hours. If the animals are weak or not eating well, you may need to feed them more often until they gain their strength and eat vigorously.

When full, woodchucks normally stop eating. Their stomachs should feel full and rounded--not tight. Remember, it is just as unhealthy to overfeed an animal as it is to underfeed it.

Following each feeding, rub each infant's belly and genital areas with a warm, damp cloth. This usually stimulates the baby to urinate or have a bowel movement--but don't worry if it doesn't work every time. Discontinue the rubbing after a minute or so whether or not it has eliminated. This activity can be discontinued altogether once the animals begin to eliminate on their own. This usually occurs by the time the woodchucks' eyes have opened.

Even though the woodchucks are being fed formula and their eyes are still closed, add fresh greens (e.g., clover, dandelion greens, alfalfa) with soil daily to the living quarters. It is important for the woodchucks to become used to the smell and texture of their food source.

The woodchucks' eyes will open sometime around the third week of their life. At this point, they will begin to show an interest in the greens in their environment and may nibble some. Continue to offer the formula every 4 hours until the woodchucks begin to refuse the formula because they have had their fill on the vegetation. Although most of the woodchucks' liquid needs will be met by the vegetation, supply the animals with a water source (dish or hanging pet water bottle). The formula can be discontinued when the animals are eating a natural diet.

It is important to provide greens that have not been sprayed with chemicals or contaminated in any other way. It is also important to change the greens and soil daily even if none has been eaten.

RELEASING

When the woodchucks are beginning to eat on their own, move them to a larger cage where they can get exercise. Begin taking the cage outside and leaving it for several hours. Don't leave it in direct sunlight, but rather in a part sunny/part shaded area. Gradually increase the hours the animals spend outside.

When they are completely weaned and eating a natural diet, they can be moved to a larger, permanent outdoor cage. A cage that measures 8' x 8' x 4' is adequate. The outside cage should be completely predator- and escape-proof. Be sure there are water-proofed areas to allow escape from rain and include a nesting box within the large cage. Provide the woodchucks with natural landscaping in the cage, such as logs, rocks, soil areas, branches, and a water source. Do not put the food in a dish--spread it out in the cage among the natural features. At this point, human contact should be limited to the activities necessary to provide fresh greens in the morning and evening, to change the water, and to clean the cage daily to prevent spoilage. If all the greens are consumed, you might not be feeding enough. Provide enough greens so that there is a small amount left between feedings.

By the time the woodchucks are about 2 1/2 months old they probably will have been living outside and eating natural foods for at least 10 days. At this point, release can be considered. Check the weather forecast before releasing and wait for a predicted period of at least 3 days without rain or dramatic drops in temperature.

Release the woodchucks away from human habitation and away from roads. The ideal release habitat is an area that includes dry soils, open woodlands, thickets, rocky slopes, fields, and clearings. Make sure the woodchucks are well fed before they are released--there may be several days when they eat very little and will have to live off body reserves.

SQUIRRELS

(Fox, Gray, Red, Flying, and Ground)

IN THE WILD

The first squirrel litters appear in March and the second in late July or early August. Fox and Gray Squirrels have 3-5 young per litter, Red Squirrels have 1-8, Flying Squirrels have 2-6, Chipmunks have 2-8, and Gophers have 2-6. The newborn are pink, naked, blind, deaf, and toothless.

Fox and Gray Squirrels develop rather slowly--not being fully formed until about 3 weeks. The ears open after 24-28 days and the eyes after 35-42 days. The weaning process starts at about 6-7 weeks; then solid food supplements the milk diet. By 10-12 weeks, the young achieve full independence.   Their natural food includes nuts and large seeds, acorns, fruits, berries, mushrooms, new shoots and branches, and the cocoons of insects.

Some types of squirrels are hole-nesters but others build their own leaf or grass nests in trees. Study the natural history of any squirrels before raising them so as to determine the right kind of natural flooring and the right kind of shelter and habitat for your boxes and cages.

Please note that diurnal (active in the daytime) squirrels generally do not share territories well, particularly in the nesting season. Black Squirrels and Red Squirrels generally are more aggressive and may drive Fox Squirrels out of an area with limited food supplies or nest trees.   Therefore, habitat selection for releasing these species is important.

In winter, all squirrels generally den up together. As many as 15-20 Flying Squirrels have been found sleeping together (probably to keep warm) and Fox, Black, and Red Squirrels also den or nest up in groups. It is important, therefore, not to raise or release a single squirrel in an area where there are no other squirrels of that species.

WHAT TO DO FIRST

When you receive young squirrels, check each animal's temperature immediately--a squirrel's normal temperature is higher than yours, so if the animal does not feel warm, you should get the temperature back up to normal. The most efficient way is by using your own body heat--hold the animals either in your hands or under your shirt. You also can use a heating pad, with several layers of towelling separating the babies from the heat source, or a warm hot water bottle wrapped in a towel.

If a baby squirrel's skin tents when pinched, and if the squirrel is listless and weak, it is probably dehydrated. After the animal regains its normal body temperature, it should be given a small drink (only a few drops if the animal is newborn) of re-hydrating solution every 15 minutes over the next hour: 1 tsp. salt, 3 tbs. sugar in 1 quart warm water.

If you are sure the babies are warm and hydrated, prepare housing and begin a normal feeding schedule.

HOUSING

Line any small box with newspaper and then add flannel or towelling. The sides of the box must be high enough so that the baby squirrel can't climb out. Place the box in an area away from drafts and noise.

If a heating pad is used, place it outside under 1/4 to 1/3 of the box and up one side. This allows the animal to select the amount of warmth needed. If you have more than one squirrel, you can leave the heating pad off during the day and during all but cold nights after the squirrels are furred. Start the pad on low heat and use your hand to determine whether the warmth is coming through the box--it should feel warm, not hot. The temperature for the very young should be 95°F. If a light bulb is used, hang an ordinary 60-watt bulb near the box and position the light over one end of the box so that the temperature will vary from one end to the other. Be sure the squirrel can't reach the bulb and be burned. The size and depth of the box should be adjusted as the squirrels become more mobile. The bedding and newspapers should be changed daily or more often if needed. When the squirrels are fully furred (a full, bushy tail is a good indicator), remove heating devices.

As the squirrels open their eyes and ears and begin to move around, place natural twigs, leaves and grasses in the box. This is important because the first smells and touches should be of natural materials as much as possible. The first sensations recorded in the animal's memory cells should be in tune with what it will find in the wild.

FEEDING
Use 1 part of powdered formula (Esbilac or Unilact) to 3 parts of warm water. Add 3-4 drops of a liquid balanced vitamin per cup of food. If, in spite of your efforts, the baby sucks so hard that the mixture bubbles out its nose, thicken the mixture with human baby cereal. Continue to feed slowly. Pneumonia may develop if formula gets into the animal's lungs. Feed with an eyedropper, syringe, or pet-nurser bottle--depending on the size of the babies.

If the babies are pink, with no fur, or very little, and the eyes are tightly closed, feed carefully until the stomach is full and round. At this age give approximately 2 cc of formula every 2 hours, with 1 night feeding.

Stimulate each young squirrel after each feeding by rubbing its belly and genital areas with a warm, damp cloth until the animal has had a bowel movement and has urinated. Don't worry if elimination does not occur each time. Discontinue stimulation after about 60 seconds. Do this after each feeding until the eyes are fully opened.

Feed very slowly and carefully; be certain each squirrel does not develop a suck that is so hard it pulls formula into the lungs. Periodically remove the bottle, syringe, or eyedropper from the mouth to prevent a hard sucking reflex from developing and to allow the squirrel to take adequate breaths.

If a squirrel is furry all over and its eyes are still closed, it should take up to 6 cc per feeding. Feed every 4 hours during daylight hours. Now night feeding may be discontinued if the babies seem strong and healthy.

When the eyes are open, squirrels will eat 9-12 cc per feeding--every 4-5 hours during the day. Also, leave solids around for them to gnaw on--apple slices, Cheerios, unsalted nuts, berries, wheat germ, seeds, green buds, etc. Place formula in a shallow jar cap or dish so squirrels may begin to lap on their own.

As squirrels start eating solids, taper off on the formula--4 feedings a day, then 3, then 2, and finally 1. Wait about 4 days between feeding deletions. Feed weaned squirrels by scattering food on the bottom of the cage. Flying squirrels should be fed at night, other species during the day. Provide a shallow water dish with water at all times.

RELEASING

Gradually change the squirrels to a balanced diet of nuts, fruits, twigs, leaves, sunflower seeds, etc. Also, they should be in a cage large enough to allow lots of climbing for exercise. Equip the cage with several tree limbs and a nest box. As the squirrels become grown and develop a full fur coat, place outside (a gradual process beginning with warm days and working up to day and night) to allow acclimatization to outdoor temperatures and noises. Outside cages should be at least 6' x 6' x 6' for 1 squirrel. Inside cages should be at least 4' square.

If squirrels occur naturally in your area, try to release the hand-raised squirrels in your own yard. Look for a number of large trees and shrubs for cover. Once the squirrels are acclimatized, leave the cage door open so they can come and go as they wish, but continue to provide them with food and water. The cage can be on or above ground, even in a tree. Gradually the squirrels will depend less and less on you and will finally become completely independent and abandon the cage. Do not release in your yard if there are cats, dogs, or unsuitable habitat.

If you can't release the squirrels from your yard and they are eating a diet of completely natural foods, release the animals with a food supply in a site that is amply supplied with food and in a place where you've seen other squirrels. Squirrels generally should be fully released by age 12 weeks.

SPECIAL NOTES ON GROUND SQUIRRELS

Unlike the larger squirrels, ground squirrels become self-sufficient very quickly. Even tiny newborns, not much bigger than a peanut, are fully furred, agile, and startle easily. Newborns readily and easily take formula from an eyedropper. As the eyes open, they begin eating wheat germ, shelled sunflower seeds, bird feed, nuts, apple slices, and whole wheat cereal. They also learn quickly to drink from a small lid. From this point on, it will no longer be necessary to continue formula feeding.

The ideal housing unit for ground squirrels is gerbil caging with a maze of tubal runways which simulate their natural burrows. Given the opportunity, they establish separate sleeping, eating, and toilet areas. However, if a Habitrail (brand name) unit is not available to you, a box is satisfactory. Give the squirrels nesting-type materials to form their own "bedroom" and try to allow them separate areas for other needs. Release them as soon as they are eating adequately on their own. If possible, leave a small box with food in the field for them (hidden in tall grass). This gives some food and shelter until they can find an old burrow or dig their own. It is especially important to release them when the weather forecast is without rain or dramatic drops in temperature for the next 3-4 days.

Ground squirrels do not become "tame" as larger squirrels may and will retain a startle reflex. For this reason, they should be handled and disturbed as little as possible. They have been known to "play dead" as do Opossums. A ground squirrel, if frightened, will look and react as if dead except its body will be limp rather than stiff. If a healthy, normal animal plays dead, it should simply be left alone--it will recover completely on its own.

TIPS FROM VOLUNTEERS

If a young squirrel gets bloated, immerse its body in warm water for about 5 minutes and stroke the abdominal and anal areas. Dry the baby carefully and within several hours the bloat should disappear. Bloat may be an indication that you are over-feeding, or of intestinal blockage or infection.

If possible, try to raise squirrels in groups of 2 or more—squirrels do not seem to do well alone.

Male squirrels may suck on each other's penises. Although this is normal, watch to see that a penis does not get swollen or bloody. If this happens, separate the males until the penis heals.

Don't let squirrels become accustomed to household pets.

If the squirrel has frequent diarrhea, feed it small amounts of a flat cola drink with honey or other re-hydration fluid in between regular feedings. Also, try mixing the regular formula with 4 parts of water rather than 3.

TIPS ON MANGE

Loss of hair may be a result of a sunshine (vitamin D) deficiency or the result of mange. Mange is a loss of hair caused by a small mite on the skin of the squirrel. (See **MANGE** section in **DISEASES OF MAMMALS** chapter; consult a veterinarian for treatment of mange.)

One treatment method is to wash the animal thoroughly with Mycodex or a good commercial flea and tick shampoo. Lather the shampoo in well and keep it on for 5 minutes before rinsing. Repeat the treatment daily for at least 3 days and dust the cage and bedding with flea and tick powder. Very young squirrels should not be dusted or bathed in any solution containing pesticides because the pesticide may damage the nervous system and the animal may die of convulsions.

MICE

IN THE WILD

The Deer Mouse (species raised by the Nature Center volunteers) is the most common of the several species of mice in this area. The adults have long tails, large eyes and ears, pure white bellies and feet, and gray, fawn, or brown upper parts. They are 6-8" in total length.

The regular breeding season starts in March or April and continues until fall. The gestation period is 21-27 days with litters of 1-8. Newborns are naked, blind, and deaf and have pink, transparent, wrinkled skin. Their total length is 1-1 1/2". Pigmentation in the skin shows after 2 days, and after 3 days, hair starts to grow and the ears unfold. The eyes open after about 12-17 days and the young are weaned in 22-37 days. Their diet consists of all kinds of seeds, thin-shelled nuts, berries, small fruits, twigs, and insects. The Deer Mouse is primarily a nocturnal animal and usually lives in wooded areas.

HOUSING

Newborn mice should be put in a small, deep box with a heating pad (turned on low) outside and under about 1/3 of the box. Put newspapers in the box; make a small tent out of some of them for the mice to hide under. Clean the box often. When the mice have their eyes open and are fully furred, the heating pad can be removed. As the mice grow, watch to see that they don't chew their way out of the box if it is made of cardboard.

FEEDING

Mice should be fed a mixture of Unilact or Esbilac formula and water, 3 parts of warm water to 1 part of dry formula. Mix 3-4 drops of vitamins per cup of formula. Feed them about every 3 hours with an eyedropper until their stomachs are rounded. They will stop eating when they are full. Be careful the mouse doesn't aspirate the formula into its lungs. Stimulate each young after each feeding by rubbing its belly and genital areas with a warm damp cloth until the animal has had a bowel movement and has urinated. Discontinue stimulation after a minute whether the mouse has eliminated or not. Do this after each feeding until their eyes have fully opened.

When mice start to open their eyes, put some bird feed, nuts, cheese, apple pieces, or raw oatmeal in the box. Also put a small dish (a jar lid works well) of water in the box. When you see that they are eating the food in the box, cut down on the formula feedings gradually over a period of several days.

When the mice are fully furred and at least half grown and eating seeds and other natural foods, they can be released in a wooded or grassland area. Check the weather forecast before releasing and wait for at least 3 days without rain or dramatic drops in temperature. Release in thick grasses and shrubs where there is food and shelter. Leave a small pile of seeds and nuts at the release site.

MUSKRATS

IN THE WILD

The muskrat is well adapted for an aquatic existence and spends its life in or near water. Although it uses a wide variety of aquatic habitats, such as lakes, streams, ponds, marshes, and sloughs, water depth is critical for optimum conditions. It should be 4-10' or 12' deep so the water does not freeze to the bottom, yet shallow enough to support the muskrat's primary food, aquatic vegetation.

The muskrat has two basic types of dens or houses. In ponds and marshy areas it builds a house on a log, stump, or clump of willows, usually situated near the edge of emergent vegetation and deep water. Another type of home consists of a den burrowed into the bank at water's edge, usually with an underwater entrance. Bank dens are apparently preferred for a nursery.

Breeding takes place usually between March and September and often 2 or 3 litters are produced. The litter size ranges from 2-8.

The blind, naked, and helpless newborns weigh less than an ounce. Their eyes open after 14-16 days; the young are then able to swim, dive, and climb. At this age, the young muskrats nurse as well as forage some on their own. They are weaned after 21-28 days, becoming independent at about 1 month of age.

The adult muskrat has a head and body length of 11-15" with an 8-11" tail. The mature muskrat weighs from 26-53 ounces.

Muskrats are herbivorous. They eat various portions of aquatic plants, especially shoots, roots, bulbs, tubers, stems, and leaves. They commonly dig for food in sod on lake and pond bottoms. Soil itself forms a portion of their diet. In Michigan, the major sources of nutrition for muskrats are cattail, bulrush, corn, duckweed, willow, poplar, maple, acorn, sweet clover, white clover, and pond weed. Muskrats are active during the day, but feed mostly at night. A muskrat may consume as much as 1/3 of its weight a day.

WHAT TO DO FIRST

When you receive young muskrats, check the temperature immediately--a muskrat's normal temperature is higher than yours, so if the animals do not feel warm, you should get the temperature back to normal. The most efficient way is by using your own body heat--hold the animals either in your hands or under your shirt to transmit your own body heat to the chilled muskrats. You can also warm the young by placing them on a heating pad set on a low temperature or on a hot water bottle wrapped in towelling. Warm the baby slowly and never try to feed until the body temperature is normal.

If the skin tents when it is gently pinched, the young are probably dehydrated. After the muskrats regain their normal body temperature, they should be given a small amount of re-hydrating solution every 15 minutes for the next hour. Re-hydration solution: 1 tsp. salt, 3 tablespoons sugar in a quart of warm water. After you are sure the young are warm and hydrated, prepare housing and begin a normal feeding schedule.

HOUSING

The baby muskrats should be placed in a small nesting box (the size will vary depending on the number of young, but usually a berry box or butter container is about the right size) lined with soft bedding. The nesting box is then placed in a larger box to keep the babies from crawling out.

If the eyes are not yet opened, heat should be provided. If a heating pad is used, place the pad outside and under 1/4 to 1/3 of the box and up one side. This allows warmth when needed but escape if it is too warm. Start the pad on low heat and use your hand to test the warmth coming through the nesting box--it should feel warm, not hot. The temperature for the very young muskrats should be about 90°F.

If a light bulb is used, hang an ordinary 60-watt bulb near the box and position the light over one end of the box so the temperature will vary from one end to the other. Make sure the animals cannot reach the bulb and be burned.

Some rehabilitators use the light during the day and the heating pad at night so the animals get a sense of sunshine and darkness.

The heat is removed when the muskrats are fully furred and seem to be spending most of their time away from the heat. This usually will occur when the eyes first open. After you have removed the heat, check to be sure the animals are maintaining their body heat.

Grasses, clover, cattails, and other natural foods are put in the box even with the very young so the animals begin the process of recognizing the smell and feel of the natural diet. Change this food daily.

FEEDING

Before feeding the muskrats, be sure they are fully awake. Sometimes it helps to gently massage the animals until they appear fully awake and alert. This massaging motion also may stimulate a suck reflex in young muskrats.

Use 1 part Esbilac or Unilact to 3 parts warm water. Add 3-4 drops of pet vitamins to each cup of formula. Feed the warmed formula to the infants with an eyedropper, syringe, or pet-nurser approximately every 4 hours. If the animals are weak or not eating well, you may need to feed them more often until they gain their strength and eat vigorously.

Normally muskrats will stop eating when they are full. The stomach should feel full and rounded but not tight and distended. Remember, it is just as unhealthy to overfeed animals as it is to underfeed them.

Following each feeding, rub the belly and genital areas with a warm, damp cloth. This usually stimulates the young to urinate or have a bowel movement--but don't worry if it doesn't work every time. Discontinue the rubbing after a minute or so whether or not they have eliminated. The muskrats no longer need stimulation after the eyes have opened or if you notice that they are eliminating between feedings on their own.

Even though the muskrats are being fed formula and the eyes are still closed, add fresh aquatic plants with soil daily to the living quarters. It is important for the muskrats to become used to the smell and texture of their future food. Change this food daily.

The muskrats' eyes will open sometime around the second week of life. At this point, they will begin to show an interest in the vegetation you have put in their environment and may nibble some. Continue to offer the formula every 4 hours until the muskrats begin to refuse the formula because they have had their fill of the vegetation. Although most of the liquid needs will be met by the vegetation, supply the animals with a water source anyway. The formula can be discontinued when the muskrats are eating a natural diet.

It is important to provide vegetation similar to what they will find in the release area you have selected. It is also important to be sure the vegetation has not been sprayed with chemicals. Remove all uneaten food at the end of each day. Because muskrats are nocturnal feeders, add the fresh food in the evening rather than in the morning.

RELEASE
Once the animals' eyes have opened and they have begun nibbling the natural foods that are being offered, move them to an outside release site. For the first couple of days, leave them outside only for a few hours. Gradually increase the time until they are spending all day and all night outside.

An ideal release cage is one that is about 6' x 6' x 4' and placed on the shore of the water into which they eventually will be released. One end of the box is mounded with fresh soil into which is nestled the nesting box. About 1/4 of the cage is in the water. Plan the cage to allow for changes in water depth--be sure a storm or windy day won't result in swamping the nesting mound. The cage must be predator-proof and have a top and 2 sides solid to protect the animals from rain, wind, and too much sun.

When the muskrats are weaned, put their natural diet in the release cage. The cattails, bulrush, and clover are put on the soil mound and the duckweed in the water. Six weaned muskrats will eat a bushel of plants a day. The uneaten food is removed and the fresh food is added every evening.

By 5 weeks of age, the muskrats should be eating a totally natural diet, swimming well, and ready to be independent of you.

Carefully select your release site. Keep in mind such factors as the number of muskrats already in the habitat, whether or not there are trappers active in that area, amount of motor boat activity, depth of the water, and availability of feeding and nesting sites.

After the muskrats have been living outside and eating on their own for a week, they are ready to release. Check the weather forecast before releasing and wait for a predicted period of at least 3 days without rain or dramatic drops in temperature. Make sure the animals are well fed before they are released--there may be several days when they eat very little and must live off body reserves. Release them in the evening near their food source.

RABBITS

IN THE WILD

Just prior to birth of a litter, the female prepares a nest which may be underground or in a concealed, grass-lined cavity under vegetation. She lines the den using fur plucked from her abdomen. The newborns (1-8) are 4" long, born with their eyes closed and their ears flat against their heads. They are not born with fur, but within a week they have a full coat. The eyes open 6-10 days after birth.

The babies are nursed about twice a day, then are otherwise left to grow under the watchful eye of the adult nearby for about 2 weeks. Baby cottontails leave the nest at 2-3 weeks and learn to nibble tender grass shoots nearby. They leave the nest for good when they are about 3-4 weeks old. They may remain in the nest area.

The question is often asked: Will the mother rabbit return if the nest has been disturbed?

We believe that there is no absolute rule followed by mother rabbits. The maternal instinct is very strong and they probably will return to feed 2-3 times within a 24-hour period if the nests have not been drastically disturbed. There have been recorded observations of mother rabbits returning to care for very young rabbits when the nest was mildly disturbed and there have been observations of abandoned young after some mild or severe disturbance of the nest. We tell people this and urge them to stay away and leave the nest alone for 24 hours before making a decision. If young are warm and healthy at this point, the mother has been returning. If the young feel cold and appear thin or dehydrated, she probably is not and it is time to bring the bunnies to a rehabilitator.

WHAT TO DO FIRST

When you receive a litter of rabbits, their temperature is immediately important. A rabbit's normal temperature is higher than yours, so if the babies do not feel warm, you should get the temperature back up to normal as soon as possible. Raise the temperature slowly by placing the babies in a small box lined with soft towelling and place a heating pad (set on "warm") under the box; or use a hot water bottle wrapped in towelling. Leave the babies there until they feel warm to the touch.

If the bunnies' skin tents (when pinched lightly) and they appear weak and listless, the babies are probably dehydrated. After they regain their normal body temperature, they should be given a small drink (just a few drops if they are newborn) of re-hydrating solution every 15 minutes over the first hours: 1 tsp. salt, 3 tbs. sugar in 1 quart warm water.

If you are sure that the babies are warm and hydrated, then proceed to prepare housing and begin a normal feeding schedule.

HOUSING

Line any small box with newspaper and then add flannel or towelling. The sides of the box must be higher than for other mammals because even baby rabbits can jump very high. Place the box in an area away from drafts and in a quiet place because bunnies are easily frightened.

If a heating pad is used, place the pad outside and under 1/4 to 1/3 of the box and up one side. This allows warmth when needed but escape if too warm. Start the pad on low heat and use your hand to feel the warmth coming through the box--the box should feel warm, not hot. The temperature for the very young should be 95°F.

If a light bulb is used, hang an ordinary 60-watt bulb near the box and position the light over one end of the box so that the temperature will vary from one end to the other. Feel the bunnies periodically to make sure the light bulb is keeping them warm. If not, switch to a heating pad.

The size and depth of the box should be adjusted as the rabbits become larger and better jumpers. Rabbits can jump surprisingly high at a very young age. Hang towels around the sides of the box to prevent the rabbits from breaking their necks when they jump. As they mature, place fresh clover and unsprayed grass in the box so that the first sights and smells will be natural. The box should be cleaned twice a day! The heat can be removed when the bunnies are fully furred and beginning to eat on their own.

FEEDING

Use 1 part powdered formula (Esbilac or Unilact) to 3 parts warm water plus 2 parts heavy cream. Add 2-3 drops of balanced liquid vitamins per cup of formula. Rabbits eat better if the formula is warmed.

Feed the babies with an eyedropper, syringe, or pet-nurser bottle--depending on the size and age of the rabbits.

There is disagreement on how often to feed baby rabbits. Some authorities recommend not feeding them more often than every 6 hours. Animal care volunteers have had success, when the bunnies' eyes are closed, by feeding them about every 2-3 hours from 7 AM to 11 PM. The time between feedings is lengthened as rabbits eat more per feeding. We have also had success feeding every 6 hours. A poor eater may require more feedings a day than a vigorous eater. Some volunteers have slowly worked up to 6 hours between feedings with healthy vigorous bunnies. With pink, hairless bunnies, feed about 1/2 cc of warm formula every 3 hours. Bunnies with their eyes tightly closed and ears flat to their head will eat about 2 eyedroppers-full (approximately 2 cc) per feeding. The amount increases as their size and weight increase. The stomach should be full and round--not tight. The amount will also vary depending on how often the bunnies are fed. Feed slowly so that the formula is not aspirated into the lungs. Food in the lungs increases susceptibility to pneumonia.

Do not be discouraged if bunnies do not feed well at the first 1 or 2 feedings. Rabbits have nervous systems which do not easily adapt to new situations or to changes. That hard syringe or eyedropper in the mouth is difficult to learn to associate with food. Being held in a human hand is also a difficult adjustment as are your odors and sounds. Be patient and persistent. Some volunteers acquire an extra box and sit on the floor at feeding time. They feed 1 bunny, place it in the extra box (so as to be able to tell which they have fed) and do the same for each bunny in that litter. They then feed the bunnies in reverse order from the extra box back to the nesting box. This procedure is done to make certain each bunny is fed twice and gets 2 chances to fill its stomach.

Some volunteers have reported that even bunnies with their eyes closed will nibble on fresh greens (clover, wild carrot greens, dandelion greens, etc.). So, we recommend adding fresh, unsprayed greens to the box daily even if the bunnies' eyes are closed. At this point, however, continue with regular formula feeding until the eyes have opened.

Bunnies over 7 days old do not need stimulation after each feeding in order to defecate and urinate--they will eliminate on their own. Bunnies less than a week old, however, do need to be stimulated after each feeding.

When the eyes are open, continue adding lots of fresh new grass and weeds, slices of apple, dandelion greens, Queen Anne's Lace tops, clover, Cheerios, and wheat germ to the floor of the box each day. Place some formula in a shallow jar cap with added yogurt (with berries) in order to help prevent intestinal bacterial diseases. Gradually, over a period of several days, eliminate formula feedings as the rabbits start eating on their own. Although bunnies get some moisture from the greens, it is advisable to add a small jar cap of water to the box after weaning.

The greens should be picked twice a day--morning and evening. Be sure the vegetation is free from any toxic sprays. Commercial rabbit pellets can be added also. Eliminate the formula when you are certain the bunnies are filling up on the natural foods. You may not actually see them eating but indications that they are include: seeing pieces of grass in the corners of their mouths; noticing the difference between how much natural food you put in and how much is left; noticing bites taken from a piece of apple; recognizing that a rabbit's tummy is rounded when no formula has been used for 4 or more hours; and a disinterest in formula.

PREPARATION FOR RELEASE

When the rabbits are completely independent of the formula, put them in an outdoor pen with wire on the bottom of the cage that is covered with soil. The wire must be fairly small gauge because rabbits can squeeze through very small openings. Try putting the rabbits out first just during the day and then at night when it isn't too chilly. They should have a nesting box within the larger cage. Be certain there is an area providing shelter from the weather. Continue fresh greens and water inside the cage daily. Create a natural shelter for hiding by simulating a small log pile, a thick grass pile, etc.

Release the rabbits in a location where there are plenty of grazing areas plus wooded areas for shelter. Release away from humans, dogs, and cats. Once a rabbit is released, it probably won't come back to a release site (as squirrels and other mammals do).

An appropriate release age is 3-5 weeks. Do not keep healthy rabbits longer than this. Even though they are not full-grown, they are ready for release and do not do well in captivity after 5 weeks.

TIPS FROM ANIMAL CARE VOLUNTEERS

If a bunny becomes bloated, put its bottom in warm water and gently massage its stomach for about 5 minutes. Dry very carefully and return it to its box. Do not chill. Within a couple of hours, the bloat should disappear. If it does not, decrease feedings temporarily or try diluting the formula 4 to 1, instead of 3 to 1 as described in the **FEEDING** section of this chapter.

Rabbits startle very easily, so be very very careful when handling them. They have injured themselves jumping suddenly from a volunteer's hands. Note illustration for appropriate feeding position. Check position of rabbit's forefeet and head when held.

Check the weather forecast before releasing the rabbits and wait for a prediction of at least 3 days without rain or dramatic drops in temperature.

It is much easier to raise rabbits in groups of 2 or more.

The white spot on a rabbit's head is a good indicator of "release age." When the white spot disappears, the rabbit should be old enough to be on its own. However, some rabbits are ready before the spot has disappeared.

Baby rabbits seem to like being covered with a soft piece of material until they are eating on their own--their natural instincts are to be under or inside a shelter. As they mature, they need to get into logs or grasses.

Self-feeding rabbits often will stop eating if there is any noise in the room or if they are being looked at.

WHITE-TAILED DEER

IN THE WILD

The White-tailed Deer, the species native to midwestern United States, is one of the most adaptable animals in the world. Its range extends from the southern tip of Hudson Bay well into South America. Although preferring woodlands and thickets alternating with open meadow and sunny forest glades, deer have been found in cities including within the shadows of the skyscrapers of New York City, in the desert, jungle, and marshes of the world. The tail, tan on top and white underneath, flips directly upward and acts as a danger signal to the rest of the herd when a predator approaches.

Male deer grow antlers which are bony structures attached to the frontal bones of the head. New antlers begin to grow in April, are nurtured by a complex network of blood vessels bringing nutrients. Antler growth in late summer and fall is related to the production of testosterone. When testosterone no longer is produced, nutrients are no longer sent to the antlers, they harden, and the velvet is rubbed off, leaving shining weapons to be used during sparring activities during the rutting season.

White-tails breed in Autumn, particularly during the first 2 weeks in November. They have a gestation period of about 7 months. Young deer of about 6-8 months of age are capable of breeding. Although 1 fawn may be carried, in older deer there are usually twins or 3 young. Fawns are spotted and born in May or June.

Healthy adult deer may live for more than 5 years, although the average age is 3-5 years.

The White-tailed Deer are both browsers and grazers. They eat a variety of vegetation, depending on their location in the world. They select the most nutritious food available if given a choice. Foods include most green plants or types of browse (clover, Queen Anne's Lace, ferns, grasses), tender leaves, shoots, and twigs (birch, maple, flowering dogwood, oak), fruits, mushrooms, acorns, agricultural crops (corn, alfalfa, soybeans, green beans, apples, etc.), and in winter they may be fed hay.

Deer are herd animals and tend to "yard-up" along river bottoms and sheltered places during winter. What may appear to be a loose herd is actually made up of several family groups which, if scattered, will regroup into their families when danger is past. They should not be raised alone.

Deer can carry a number of parasites and diseases. Some, like tuberculosis and aspergillosis, can be transmitted to humans.

WHAT TO DO FIRST

When fawns are received in a rehabilitation program, the temperature is immediately important. It is normally higher than yours, so if the fawns do not feel warm, take the temperature with a rectal thermometer. Normal body temperature is about 98°F. To raise the body temperature back to normal, use one of the following methods (depending on the size of the animal). Younger fawns may be held on one's lap, next to the human body heat, or wrapped in a warm blanket and placed in a large box set on a heating pad with towelling or newspaper between the fawn and pad to protect from over-heating. Older fawns will be frightened and difficult to hold, so if they are cold, they should be placed in a room with a temperature of above 75°F to warm up. Most fawns and older deer have good fur coats and are used to being outside, so unless the animals are very ill, they need not be indoors.

If the deer seem weak and listless and the skin "tents" up when pinched instead of quickly returning to normal position, they may be dehydrated. Feed 2-3 cups of re-hydrating solution every 15-20 minutes for the first 1-6 hours. (Re-hydrating solution can be made from 1 tsp. salt, 3 tbs. sugar in 1 quart warm water with vitamins or Nutrical added.) Use a large eyedropper, syringe, or if the fawns are older, a turkey baster. Straddle the deer or

86

hold it in a position where it cannot jerk or jump away; and gently push the feeding utensil into the mouth. If the deer will not allow the utensil in its mouth, gently slide the end of the instrument into the side of the mouth and carefully and slowly drip solution onto the back of the tongue. Stroke the throat gently to stimulate swallowing if the fawn is not getting liquid into its stomach. When the fawns have revived, utilize milk formula.

HOUSING

Healthy fawns should be kept outdoors in a cage or fenced area large enough for exercise and containing natural-growing grasses and weeds. As deer mature, they can jump very high, so cage wiring should be 8-10' high, thus confining the deer until they are ready for release. The cage should contain a weather-proof shelter with 3-4 walls to protect the deer from severe weather when very young. The floor of the shelter should be covered with a thick straw layer and cleaned frequently. As the deer mature, the shelter door should be left open so that they can move in and out at will.

FEEDING

The milk preferred by staff for fawns at the Nature Center is goat's milk. If goat's milk cannot be found at a large grocery store or nearby goat farmer, then Lamb Replacer or Foal-Ac are the next best formulas. If these two are not available, then calf-replacer may be used. It should be noted that all artificial milk replacers (Foal-Ac, calf-replacer) generally cause diarrhea in deer. Goat's milk has caused no diarrhea or other upset to the digestive system of deer in our experience over the past 14 years. If lamb replacer, Foal-Ac, calf replacer, or other artificial milks are used, mix according to directions on the package and add several drops of a balanced vitamin formula to each cup of milk. If goat's milk is utilized, it may be used without additives, or in a formula of 2/3 goat's milk mixed with 1/3 Lamb Replacer (to increase fat content).

Milk should be heated to body temperature before feeding. Feeding utensils which work best include: baby bottle for young fawns up to 3 weeks old; calf or lamb nipple placed on the end of a pop bottle for fawns older than 3 weeks. Some calf nursing bottles are appropriate if they have long, flexible nipples. It is difficult to teach fawns to nurse from a nursing bottle because the temperature and texture are so different from those of the mother's teat. Young, small fawns may be encouraged to suck by dribbling a few drops on the nose or end of the tongue or by gently inserting the bottle into the mouth and holding it firmly until the fawn begins to suck.

Fawns older than 2-3 weeks are fairly wild and often will struggle when the bottle is inserted into their mouths. If all else fails, put pressure on both corners of the mouth with your thumb and forefinger and insert the bottle into the mouth. Hold the bottle firmly and squeeze milk down the back of the throat until the fawns begin to drink. Stroke the throat gently to stimulate swallowing reflexes. You may have to go through this procedure the first few times you feed just to get enough milk into the fawns to keep them going. Then begin a more gentle approach to feeding for the fawns' sake and yours. Once fawns become accustomed to associating the bottle with food, they generally will be approachable when feeding time arrives and you can hold the bottle out in front of you where they can see it.

Fawns may be taught to drink formula from a bucket or pan with sides at least 6" high. The earlier fawns are taught to do this, the better. Fawns that lap on their own early do not have a strong association with humans for food and grow faster because they may eat at will (similar to nursing in the wild) instead of by a schedule. To teach the fawns to lap, gently press the noses into the pan of milk several times before a feeding occurs. As the fawns lick the milk off the face repeatedly, they come to look to the pan for food. Another technique is to place the empty bottle with nipple sideways into the pan with the milk. The deer will attempt to lick or suck the bottle, get their tongue and lips into the milk and learn to drink on their own. This should be practiced in place of 1-2 feedings each day until the fawns are definitely drinking on their own. Bottle feeding may be discontinued at that point. Healthy fawns should be fed every 4-5 hours, taking 1-2 full pop bottles of formula per feeding at the age of 2 weeks and up. Weak fawns should be warmed, re-hydrated, then fed about every 2 hours until they regain their strength.

As fawns begin getting their teeth, make certain that fresh grass, weeds, and perhaps ground corn or whole grains are available for them. As you see them begin to nibble natural foods, decrease the number of feedings by 1 per day over a period of about a week. Place a water bucket in the shelter and make fresh water and food available several times each day. A bucket with formula may be kept in the shed until the fawn is weaned. It is highly important that fawns have natural foods available to them to develop the proper stomach bacteria for digesting natural foods. Deer fed solely on hay and cultivated grains do not develop the bacteria in their stomachs necessary for digesting natural foods and can starve when released.

Deer do not have gall bladders. Deer are ruminants--as deer browse, fresh food is partly masticated, passed into the stomach pouch (rumen or paunch) where the food softens and soaks and from which it is regurgitated at will to be chewed in the form of a cud. After it has been chewed, it is re-swallowed and passed directly to other parts of the stomach for further digestion.

SPECIAL NOTES

When fawns are not raised on goat's milk, but placed on substitute formulas, they almost always get diarrhea, which is sometimes runny yellow or black. This may continue, if the fawns' systems cannot adjust to the formula, until the fawns are weaned to natural foods. Proper medicines from a veterinarian who deals with cows and horses can help slow down or partly solidify the bowel movement. Make certain the fawns do not dehydrate during this time by providing water and re-hydration solution by syringe bottle.

As with other mammals, the mother licks the young to stimulate urination and bowel movements. Stimulate the young after each feeding by rubbing under the tail and genital areas with a warm damp cloth until the animals have had a bowel movement. Discontinue this after a minute or 2 whether or not the deer have eliminated. Most young fawns urinate on their own very early, but need stimulation to have a bowel movement until 4-5 weeks of age.

KEEP HUMAN CONTACT TO A MINUMUM, PREFERABLY ONLY DURING FEEDING TIME, TO PREVENT THE FAWNS FROM IMPRINTING ON HUMANS.

A number of deer injured by dogs or run over by hay mowers or combines are brought to the Center each spring. Many die of the shock and trauma or infection to which they have been subjected; others do not recover from anesthetics. A veterinarian experienced in wildlife care can make a great difference in the success of anesthetic use and operations on injured deer.

RELEASING

Deer should always be released in large areas away from people, especially farmers and hunters, and away from roads. Many times they become excessively tame when hand-raised and lose all instinctive fear of humans. Occasionally during the first week of release, deer raised at the Nature Center have walked up to hunters on the surrounding area in spite of our best efforts to minimize human contact with them during raising.

Two methods may be utilized in releasing.

Method A

If the pen the deer have been raised in is near or in a large woods or thicket area with fields or marshes nearby, the door of the pen may be opened to allow the deer to come and go at will. Usually deer have little difficulty in foraging on their own, but may return to the shelter for security until they make contact with a wild herd. Be certain that the pen does not trap the deer for wandering dogs. Also, human contact with deer should be eliminated after releasing.

Method B

When the deer are ready for release, they may be transported to large, suitable release areas. This method causes trauma to the deer because they are not accustomed to riding in trucks or vans. Unless confined in a padded container, they may cause themselves injury during transport. Try to locate a wild herd of deer ahead of time and release the deer near herd signs, such as a trail, if possible. Do not release near farm crops or gardens because deer may cause crop damage.

Deer should be released in August or after they have been weaned. It is preferable to wait until most of their spots disappear and they have gone through a molt to obtain adult tawny coats. They may be close to adult size or 3/4 grown at release time. Some of our deer have jumped the fence in early August when they still had spots and have done very well going wild. Deer should be released well ahead of the hunting season so they may join a wild herd, regain fear of humans, and locate sheltered thickets for hiding. They should be released no later than 3 1/2 or 4 months of age, if healthy.

BIRDS

GENERAL CARE OF ORPHANED BIRDS

MAKE CERTAIN THAT YOUNG BIRDS BROUGHT TO YOU ARE ACTUALLY ORPHANED. If you
find baby birds that can't fly, put them back into the nest (if you can find
it) or make a "foster" nest in a tree near or under where the original nest
was.

If you find baby birds on the ground that are feathered, are calling, are
hopping around, and can barely fly, they probably have just fledged (been
coaxed off the nest by the parent birds). Keep predators away and get out of
the area so the parents can locate and take care of them. Young birds will
not be rejected just because they have been touched by humans. Allow 12-20
hours for the adult birds to locate their young before making a decision to
pick up the bird and take it to a rehabilitation center.

If you find orphaned ducks or Killdeer (or other shorebirds), make an attempt
to locate the mother and the rest of the brood. Release the young nearby and
leave the area so the mother and young may find each other by their calls.

SUPPLIES NEEDED

You will need: toothpicks, coffee stirrers or small spoons, food, room
thermometer, heating pad and light bulb, log book, eyedroppers, medicines,
plastic laundry bottles cut in half, berry boxes, cottage cheese containers
(or anything that will make a suitable, make-shift nest), and plastic laundry
baskets inverted on each other to form a secure holding cage, or boxes with
netting or wire for the top. Use natural history books as references.

HOUSING

Don't save the original nest that the birds have come in because it may have
lice, mites, or other parasites in it. Place the birds in a small bowl or
berry box lined with several layers of puffed-up tissue or cut-up diapers for
body support. Do not use grass--dry grass is too hard to keep clean and
fresh grass is too cold and damp. Cover the birds with an opened facial

91

tissue or wash cloth or towel with holes cut in it (to copy the feeling of the parent bird lying on top of the young). Place the bowl in a larger box or 2 inverted laundry baskets for a cage and attach perches through the walls for the birds to use as they develop. One laundry basket with cardboard top or 2 large laundry baskets tied upside down on each other will make a safe cage (see sketches below).

If you have only 1 bird in the nest, place a small mirror or mirrors in the cage with the single bird. This seems to help the bird to imprint on its own species and also apparently gives the bird some competition for food.

Keep the nest warm by using a heating pad or a 60-watt electric light bulb hung near the nest. Use a thermometer to check the temperature of the cage. It should be about 99°-100°F.

If a heating pad is used, place it outside under half of the box and be sure to monitor the temperature carefully, because the bird may become overheated if it cannot move away from the heat. Make certain that heat circulates up around the birds. If a light bulb is used for heat, use no more than a 60-watt bulb and place it so that a 95°F temperature is maintained at the nest. When the baby's feathers start to emerge from their protective sheaths, the birds are beginning to be able to control their own body temperature and the nest temperature can be decreased 5°F a week until 70°F is reached.

Keep the heat available as long as the birds sit near it and use it for warmth. When the birds are fully feathered, remove the source of heat.

Place young birds in a cage with more space until they are ready for outside. Use as large a box or cage as possible because as the birds get older they can fly and should exercise. Some birds (especially those not hand-raised) may harm themselves when kept in a conventional (canary or parakeet) bird cage. They should instead be kept in a box or other container that does not allow feathers to slip through the bars and become stripped. Keep the cage in a quiet place and away from drafts. Do not put water in with young birds until they are fully feathered, because they may get into it, get wet, and become chilled. Mist (spray lightly with water from a spray bottle) birds once a day when they are fully feathered. This helps water-proof the bird, and starts the preening reflex. Remember--birds fly primarily horizontally, not vertically. Cages or flight pens should be long instead of high. Laundry baskets can be used for housing of nestlings and fledged birds under 2-3 weeks of age, depending on the species.

Outside cages or flight pens also should be long rather than high and off the ground because birds feel secure higher up. A minimum size flight cage for any song bird should be 8' long, 8' wide, and 6' deep. A cage this size can provide 6-8 birds enough room to learn to fly well and forage for natural food. If a cage is overcrowded, disease can become a serious concern. Remember--this cage should be predator-proof.

SAMPLE RELEASE PEN FOR BIRDS

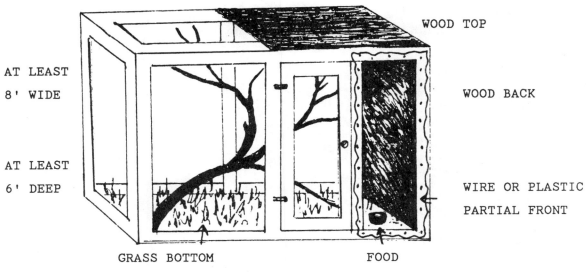

AT LEAST 8' WIDE

AT LEAST 6' DEEP

WOOD TOP

WOOD BACK

WIRE OR PLASTIC PARTIAL FRONT

GRASS BOTTOM

FOOD

AT LEAST 8' LONG

SPECIAL PROBLEMS AND CONDITIONS

BLOAT OR CONSTIPATION

When altricial baby birds eat, they usually will eliminate immediately afterward. Stools will vary depending on the species and the diet, but, in general, droppings will be somewhat solid and the color of the food, within a whitish, liquid-like sac. If the young become constipated, it usually indicates an improper diet, and both the diet and constipation must be corrected **immediately**, or the birds may die in a very short time. If stimulating the vent area with mineral oil on a Q-tip does not work, feeding the birds fruit or earthworms may loosen the stools. Small slices cut from human baby glycerine suppositories and held in the vent may also be successful.

IMPACTED VENT

Clean and soften with mineral oil on a Q-tip--this stimulates elimination.

IMPACTED CROP

Give the birds a mixture of 1 part of vinegar to 1 part water with an eye-dropper. Depending on the size of the birds, 1/4 eyedropper each 1/2 hour for 2-3 hours may be enough to loosen crop impaction. A drop of molasses or 2 of milk of magnesia maybe used also.

CRIPPLING

Pervinal has been used with some success against crippling--give 8-9 drops daily, depending on the cause. Also, heavy doses of balanced B vitamins have been successful in curing some birds of crippling caused by accident or improper nourishment.

MITES

If mites are diagnosed, cover the birds' faces with a facial tissue and spray the birds lightly with a cage bird spray for mites (from pet shops). Or the bird may be sprinkled with **CAT** flea powder. Sprinkle or spray bottom of nest and box and place clean, new nest box materials inside. Another option is to place a cat flea collar in the box.

SIGNS OF DISEASE

Birds hide sickness well, yet weaken FAST. Watch for:

1)   Change in body attitude, appearance, loss of feathers, ruffled feathers, sitting on bottom of cage, squatting on perch, listlessness, wheezing, sneezing, "clicking," gasping, etc.

2)   Change in appetite or droppings. Save a sample for examination by supervisor or veterinarian.

3)   If the birds "act sick," you can revert to the fledgling diet or favorite food for easier digestion and add energy with Nutrical either in re-hydration formula with water or as a paste (available from a veterinarian).

COLDS, RESPIRATORY PROBLEMS

Symptoms include puffiness, audible breathing, and beak opening to breathe. If your birds develop respiratory problems as a result of being chilled or from lack of food, make up a mixture of 1 crushed aureomycin tablet (Pet Mycin, etc., from pet shops) with 1-2 drops of water; or 2 drops twice a day of any general antibiotic, such as Panmycin or Tetracycline. For serious cases some volunteers have used 1 drop of Panmycin every 2 hours for 1-2 days. Do NOT attempt other medical or surgical care on your own--consult a supervisor or veterinarian.

Increase cage temperature to 80°F; a vaporizer may be helpful.

WARNINGS

Death may result from any of the following: aerosols, open water (kitchen sink, toilets), hot stoves, boiling water, cats and dogs, stringy cloths in cage, or falling.

DISEASES OF BIRDS

Although the Kalamazoo Nature Center Wild Animal Program has never had a bird with any of the following diseases, they are included here for general information. Consult a veterinarian or state wildlife biologist for treatment of any of these.

ARBOVIRUSES

These are uncommon in birds, and much like the same group of diseases in mammals. Wild birds generally carry infectious organisms without showing signs of disease. Viruses can affect the central nervous system and produce symptoms: depression, lethargy, incoordination, paralysis, and abnormal postures of head and neck. Infections are usually fatal--some effective vaccines have been developed.

NEWCASTLE DISEASE

This very contagious viral nervous, respiratory, and gastro-intestinal disease is one of the para-influenza group. The strains in America usually are pneumotropic--symptoms include leg and wing paralysis, tremors, neck contortions, coughing, and enteritis. There is no known effective treatment. Those birds which survive usually develop long-lasting immunity. Onset is very sudden and most affected birds die.

DUCK PLAGUE (Duck Enteritis)

This is an acute, contagious viral infections of ducks, geese, and swans. Symptoms include hemorrhaging, free blood in body cavities, and lesions of internal organs. Transmission is through direct contact with affected birds or contaminated environment, usually water. The incubation period is 3-7 days and death follows in 1-5 days. Symptoms include blood-stained vents, extreme thirst, nasal discharge, soiled vents, photophobia, and diarrhea. There is no known treatment and the fatality rate is high, especially in older animals.

AVIAN POX

This is similar to pox in mammals and takes 2 forms: diphtheritic (with moist lesions on mucous membranes of mouth and upper respiratory tract); and a common skin form (with lesions on unfeathered parts of body). It is usually fatal--due as much to interference with feeding, movement, and sight as to the disease itself.

SALMONELLOSIS

See **SALMONELLA** section in **DISEASES OF MAMMALS** chapter.

AVIAN CHOLERA

This infectious bacterial disease often causes septicemia; the mortality rate is high. The disease is spread by ingestion, arthropod vectors, and inhalation by scavengers. Most birds die within hours, some survive to become carriers. Treatment should be preventive rather than therapeutic.

BOTULISM

This paralytic disease from food containing toxins from anaerobic bacteria can cause paralysis and death when respiratory and cardiac muscles are affected. More frequent in late summer and early fall, outbreaks come when naturally occurring soil bacteria are released through flooding and are incubated by summer temperatures. When a large flight of ducks moves into an area, infection takes place. Symptoms include an inability to sustain flight, movement on land aided by wings, diminished muscular control, immobility of nictitating membrane, and "limberneck" posture due to cervical muscles losing tone.

Respiratory difficulties, body temperature under 100°F, and diarrhea followed by constipation are other symptoms. Recovery depends on quick diagnosis, removal of affected birds from contaminated area, and feeding fresh water and food. The best means of combatting botulism is to supply abundant fresh water and administer anti-toxin.

CHLAMYDIOSIS (Ornithosis and Psittacosis or Parrot Fever)

This is caused by bacteria occurring naturally in both mammals and birds-- pigeons are the most common host. Arthropods can be vectors (10-30% of cases) and it has been found in 139 species of birds and mammals. Most wild birds show latent signs of the disease. The most common symptoms are an exudate of an eye or nose and diarrhea with gray or rust (blood) feces. There is often some respiratory stress and little body movement. Antibiotics can successfully treat the disease in its early stages.

COCCIDIOSIS

Coccidia (500 species of protozoa) are widespread parasites of vertebrates. When the Protozoa are eaten, they spread to the lumen of the intestinal tract, causing hemorrhaging, intestinal dysfunction, diarrhea, and dehydration. Animals that survive are often retarded in growth. The best preventive treatment is to avoid crowding and maintain cleanliness. Chlamydiosis and Coccidiosis can both be spread to humans, so use care and good hygiene when working with and cleaning your birds.

ALTRICIAL BIRDS

Altricial birds are naked and blind at hatching, confined
to a nest, and unable to feed themselves or to control
body temperature for a number of days after hatching.

NEWLY HATCHED NESTLING

WHAT TO DO FIRST

Follow procedure in **GENERAL CARE OF ORPHANED BIRDS** chapter. When the birds
come to you, examine them carefully to determine their conditions.   If
healthy and **warm**, proceed with housing and feeding.

If injured, consult a supervisor or call a veterinarian.   If cold, weak, and
dehydrated, warm them first--you can kill them by feeding when they are
cold.   To warm the birds, cup them in your hands;   hold them against your
body;   place them in the nest box or bowl, cover it lightly, and place it
near a light bulb or on a heating pad turned down low, with towels between
the pad the the birds. Unfeathered birds (1 week or younger) should be kept
at a temperature of 85-90°F.   Downy birds with a few quills showing can be
kept at 80-85°F.   Birds with feather quills and small feathers can be kept at
75-80°F.   Fully feathered dry birds can be kept at room temperature.   A good
way to tell when birds no longer need artificial heat is when they fledge
from the nest--in other words, when they hop on the perch.

If the birds can lift their heads and are active after warming, feed them food mixtures listed below (see **FEEDING** section in **GENERAL CARE OF ORPHANED BIRDS** chapter). If the birds are weak and dehydrated, **carefully** place 2-4 drops of re-hydration solution (1 tsp. salt, 3 tbs. sugar in 1 quart warm water with several drops of vitamins or Metrical) into the throat **beyond** the breathing hole at the base of the tongue or on the tip of the tongue every 1/4 hour for the first 1-2 hours. When the birds begin to revive a little, feed them food formula every 30-45 minutes. Birds do not need to be fed at night unless they are very weak.

HOUSING

See **HOUSING** section in **GENERAL CARE OF ORPHANED BIRDS** chapter.

FEEDING

Most young altricial birds are fed some form of insect life, no matter what constitutes the adult diet. As they mature, they become, in general, seed-eaters, insect-eaters, or both. Many also eat berries and other fruits.

For all young altricial birds (insect-eaters and seed-eaters) use 1 of the following food mixtures as the base: Mynah Bird food, PD canned dog food (do not use any other canned dog food because it is too high in animal fat), Puppy Chow, or dry cat food. The Kalamazoo Nature Center has had the most success using 8-in-1 Mynah Bird Food as the base.

INSTRUCTIONS FOR MIXING FOOD FOR **INSECT-EATERS**

Soak 1/3 cup of dry base food in enough warm water until the mixture is the consistency of hot cereal (this will yield about a cup). To each cup, add 3-4 drops of any balanced liquid vitamin plus 2-3 drops of vitamin B-12 if you are not using Mynah Bird food with B-12 added. Add 1/2 teaspoon ground egg shell. Some volunteers also add 1/2 teaspoon oyster shell after the birds fledge. To this mixture pick 2 foods from the following list and add 1 tablespoon each: strained baby food meats, hard-boiled egg yolk, pureed raw liver, and/or pureed raw beef.

Sample Mixture #1

1 cup soaked 8-in-1 Mynah Bird Food

1 tablespoon baby beef meat

1 tablespoon baby egg yolk

3-4 drops vitamins

1/2 teaspoon ground egg shell

Sample Mixture #2

1 cup soaked Puppy Chow

1 tablespoon pureed raw liver

1 tablespoon hard-boiled egg yolk

3-4 drops vitamins

2-3 drops vitamin B-12

1/2 teaspoon ground egg shell

INSTRUCTIONS FOR MIXING FOOD FOR **SEED-EATERS**

Soak 1/3 cup of a dry base food in enough warm water until the mixture is the consistency of hot cereal (this will yield about a cup). To each cup, add 3-4 drops of any balanced liquid vitamin plus 2-3 drops of vitamin B-12 if you are not using Mynah Bird food with B-12 added. Add 1/2 teaspoon ground egg shell. Some volunteers also add 1/2 teaspoon oyster shell after the birds fledge. To this mixture select 2 foods from the following list and add 1 tablespoon each (2 tablespoons total): high-protein baby cereal, wheat germ, corn meal, oatmeal, chicken starter, applesauce, hard-boiled egg yolk, cottage cheese (fresh--discard formula with cottage cheese after 2 hours), and/or finely ground sunflower seeds.

Sample Mixture #1

1 cup 8-in-1 Mynah Bird food

1 tablespoon hard-boiled egg

1 tablespoon ground sunflower seed

3-4 drops vitamins

1/2 teaspoon ground egg shell

Sample Mixture #2

1 cup soaked puppy chow

1 tablespoon applesauce

1 tablespoon fresh cottage cheese

3-4 drops vitamins

2-3 drops vitamin B-12

1/2 teaspoon ground egg shell

When mixing food for either the seed-eater or the insect-eater, mix only enough food for 1 day. It should be prepared daily (every 2 hours if using cottage cheese). The mixtures can be frozen in ice cube trays and each section defrosted as needed.

Very young birds are often difficult to identify; however, the bird's bill may indicate whether it is a seed-eater or an insect-eater.

The seed-eater's bill is much broader and thicker at the base. If you are not sure whether your birds are insect- or seed-eaters, always use the insect-eater formula, just to be safe.

INSECT-EATER   SEED-EATER

As birds mature, sprinkle a little grit in the food or on the bottom of the cage for both insect- and seed-eaters. If the birds eat fruit in the wild, you may add fleshy fruits: chopped apples, pears, soaked raisins, grapes, or berries. Remember to add a balanced vitamin supplement to the birds' formula. Hand-raised birds can suffer from Vitamin B deficiency, causing deformed or useless legs or muscles. Remember to add 3-4 drops of a balanced vitamin supplement containing B-12 to all food formulas.

Feed young birds every 30-60 minutes all day. (Most birds are not fed in the wild after sundown.) Feed 3-4 mouthfuls per feeding or until the birds stop eating. They usually will refuse food when they are full. Gaping can be stimulated by tapping the side of the box, wiggling the nest, or making a kissing or whistling sound. Some young birds will gape when they see their nest mates gape. Use the same gaping technique consistently. Remove excess food from the bird's face and bill. Coffee stirrers, spoon handles, dry medium noodles, etc., make good feeding utensils. Birds will eliminate after feeding--check to make sure feces are firm. Never give water to young

102

birds until they can drink from a container on their own. They get enough moisture from the food formula. Do **NOT** feed birds bread or milk.

When birds are feathered and walking or hopping about, begin a transfer to natural foods and teach the bird to feed itself. An easy way to do this is always to feed birds from the same dish and stick, and place the dish with formula plus food-stick where they can see it when you do feed them--thus they see the source of the food. Place the food dish and the food-stick in the cage or box and the bird soon will learn to peck from it. Then you may gradually stop all hand feeding.

As the young birds mature, place some of the natural foods in their food dish along with mixed formula; spread some on the bottom of the cage also. Insect-eaters should receive earthworms, mealworms, flies, mosquitoes, beetles, crickets, ants, etc. Seed-eaters may receive wild bird mix, wild grains, corn, wheat, barley, oats, weed seeds, and grit (soil or sand which they use to grind seeds in their gizzards--they have no teeth!). Both may receive fruits. Continue to use formula with natural foods for a balanced diet. Place a small, shallow water dish in the cage when the birds begin to feed themselves.

Check to see how each species feeds in the wild and try to approximate those conditions when possible. For example, Horned Larks feed by pecking insects (some seeds) from open fields. Therefore, in captivity, when the birds are old enough to begin eating on their own, place some of the formula (in the formula dish with a food-stick at first) as well as natural foods on soil in the cage. The birds then will learn to associate food with the color and texture of soil. Change the soil in the cage often to bring in a new batch of soil micro-organisms and insects.

Hand-raised birds do not learn to preen their feathers as easily as wild birds do, and they do not stimulate their oil glands adequately. When the birds have fledged the nest, start lightly misting them (use spray bottle) with warm water. This procedure will help the birds learn to preen their feathers and thus stimulate the oil gland under the tail to provide the oil with which they waterproof their feathers.

When the birds are 3-5 weeks old, well-feathered, and eating on their own for the most part, place the birds in a flight cage (at least 8' x 8') out-of-doors. If the birds hatched late in the year, make sure they have been outside where they are able to see the stars at night for at least 3 weeks before the start of migration. This is especially important for nocturnal songbirds such as thrushes and warblers. Also, if birds are late-fledging males, play a tape recording of the song of that species frequently. This will help them learn songs for the breeding process the following year. It is recommended that all birds be banded by a licensed bander before release.

HORNED LARK

RELEASING

When the birds are 3-5 weeks old, well-feathered, and eating on their own, place them outdoors. Birds should be kept outdoors in the release cage for 1-2 weeks. When they are flying well, have acquired adult feathers, and are self-feeding, the door can be opened to allow them to go free, but fresh food should be placed in the cage or on top of it daily because most birds will need to come back and feed until they are able to survive completely on their own. Remember that birds should not be friendly to or imprinted on people.

Make certain that the feeding station does not act as a trap for the benefit of predators (cats, dogs, weasels, etc.). Wherever the feeding station for release is placed, birds should be able to see all around it and be able to fly quickly into brushy cover from it if threatened. If at all possible, birds should be released as near the natural habitat and food for each species as possible. For example, when raising flickers, place the cage over an anthill near a woods. Do not stop feeding until the birds have not returned for 5-7 days.

Make certain that the weather prediction is good for at least 3-4 days after release. This is important for several reasons, one of them being that hand-raised birds do not learn to preen their feathers as wild birds do, and thus do not stimulate their oil glands adequately. Because their feathers may not have acquired the proper amount of oil, during rainstorms the feathers have little protection against water and easily become completely soaked. Birds can get chilled and die. If your bird does get soaked in a rainstorm and its feathers are not repelling water, capture the bird and take it where you can dry it carefully with a hair blower set on low and release it after the storm. After some association with wild birds, most hand-raised birds learn to preen and oil their feathers properly.

An ideal situation for a release pen is an aviary. It should be large enough to allow several compatible birds to be raised together and it should have adequate flight space. Do NOT mix dissimilar species of birds together.

The materials need not be expensive. Use fine mesh wire, aviary netting, or plastic garden netting (marketed for keeping birds out of strawberries). The frame may be built from shop lumber, old tree limbs (some volunteers have bought old screen and storm doors at garage sales and taken the glass out of the frame, using several frames for the aviary).

At least one full side and part of each connecting side should be protected from wind and rain as well as 1/3 to 1/2 of the top. Use wood or some other solid material that repels water. Plastic film is not suitable for the top because, as water builds up, the plastic sags and may leak into the cage.

Remember, birds fly horizontally primarily, so the aviary should be long rather than tall. Place perches at various heights, some in the protected area and some in the open area. Perches should not be smooth because birds cannot easily grip smooth surfaces. Limbs with bark make ideal perches. The floor should be natural grass and soil, but make certain that predators cannot dig into the cage. Provide a wide, shallow dish for water and bathing and change the food and water daily. See **SAMPLE RELEASE PEN FOR BIRDS** diagram in **GENERAL CARE OF ORPHANED BIRDS** chapter.

The cage should be placed with the protected side facing the direction from which summer winds and rains blow. Sunlight must be admitted to the aviary for the birds' general health. If birds are released directly from the cage site, suitable habitat for food and protection should be nearby. The cage should be away from people, dogs, cats, cars, and other potential hazards.

THRUSHES (ROBINS, BLUEBIRDS, ETC.)

Robins and other thrushes nest in a variety of habitats—in shrubs, trees, vines, thickets, thick grasses, beams, fence posts, and buildings. Bluebirds nest in cavities and prefer old orchards or other locations where insects and fruits are plentiful, or where there are artificial predator-free nest boxes.

AMERICAN ROBIN

Usually 3-5 eggs are laid by all species of thrushes. Incubation is usually 12-14 days and the young usually leave the nest in 13-16 days. Young are coaxed out of the nest by adults and fed until they are able to survive on their own. Their diet consists of insects (beetles, caterpillars, bugs, moths, flies, cutworms, butterflies), other invertebrates (spiders, millipedes, earthworms), and fruits, both wild and cultivated (mulberry, red cedar, juniper, pokeberry, spice bush, hawthorn, mountain ash, apple, pear, raspberry, etc.).

One volunteer who has released over 400 birds states that he places mulberries, blueberries, or other wild fruit onto the floor of the aviary where the birds learn to pick up the berries after 3 days or so. This stimulates their independent feeding response and often gets them to start picking up insects. Feed young adults as many natural foods as possible and release in natural habitats as free from pesticides or lawn or field chemicals as possible.

FLYING-INSECT-EATERS

(Includes Swifts, Swallows, Nighthawks, Flycatchers)
These birds do not gape easily and may have to be force-fed.

Gently press your thumb and index finger at the corners of the mouth, press it open, and place the food carefully down the throat. Continue to feed formula with natural insects until release. These birds need to be fed every 15-20 minutes as both fledglings and adults. Most flying-insect-eaters learn to catch insects fairly quickly if given the opportunity.

Place food in the cage to attract insects, but continue to feed the birds regularly until release. These birds come back for 1-2 weeks after being released. Flying-insect-eaters must have a large flight cage so they can learn how to fly and feed at the same time.

To prepare these birds for release, one of our volunteers lines up the young flying-insect-eaters on a perch and holds the food-stick about a foot away. When they become hungry, the birds must fly out to the stick, feed in the air, and fly back to the perch. As the birds' skills improve, the distance is lengthened. This procedure is used in conjunction with providing food which attracts flying insects into the cage. Often the birds will fly in to the food-stick after release.

WARBLERS, KINGLETS, GNATCATCHERS

COMMON YELLOWTHROAT

A variety of nesting sites are used: on the ground, in conifers, in thick shrubby places, in forks of tree branches, etc. Gnatcatchers build in deciduous trees, kinglets in conifers. Warblers and gnatcatchers may lay 3-6 eggs: kinglets, 6-11 eggs. Incubation is 12-13 days and is performed mostly by the female, who is fed by the male.

Both parents feed the young. The eyes of the young open at 4-5 days. Their food is mostly insects of all types, especially small flying ants, leaf worms, locusts, gnats, weevils, beetles, bugs, lice, and non-insects such as earthworms and spiders. Kinglets and Ovenbirds may eat small berries occasionally. For raising and releasing, see **RELEASING** section in **ALTRICIAL BIRDS** chapter and **FLYING-INSECT-EATERS** and **SWIFT** sections.

SWIFTS

Chimney Swifts usually nest in chimneys or inside hollow trees in June. The nest is constructed of twigs, half-a-saucer shaped, and glued to the wall by the bird's hardened glutinous saliva. Three to 6 eggs are laid and early in life young swifts can cling to the wall or nest by use of their long, sharp toenails. Their eyes open at about 14 days and they leave the nest in about 1 month. Their natural diet is flying insects (beetles, flies, mosquitoes, etc.).

CHIMNEY SWIFT

Feed them an insect-eater's diet and transfer to their natural diet as soon as possible. Chimney Swifts gape "crazily," meaning they wave their necks wildly through the air, thus it helps to use an eyedropper and to have a quick hand to place the eyedropper in the birds' mouths. Place food in their cage to attract insects when they are able to feed themselves. Continue to supplement with regular formula every 15-20 minutes to make certain that the birds are getting enough to eat. When they are fully feathered and flying well on their own, release them from the cage. They may return for 1-2 weeks; feed them until they no longer return.

FLYCATCHERS, PHOEBES, PEWEES, KINGBIRDS

EASTERN WOOD-PEWEE

These nest in a variety of habitats: high in trees, in holes in trees, low or high in shrubs, in holes in buildings, on platforms overhanging water, on fence posts, etc. Three to 7 eggs may be laid per clutch and their incubation is 13-16 days. Flight feathers may begin to grow at 4-6 days and the young leave the nest after about 18-20 days. Their food consists primarily of insects and spiders: flies, beetles, bugs, spiders, grasshoppers, crickets, moths, butterflies, and caterpillars. Small amounts of seeds or berries may be consumed (no more than 10% of the diet). Feed insect-eater diet and supplement with insects when possible. Make sure birds are getting enough. For raising and releasing, see **RELEASING** section in **ALTRICIAL BIRDS** chapter and **FLYING-INSECT-EATERS** and **SWIFT** sections.

SWALLOWS, MARTINS

These birds may nest in a variety of places and some are named for the places they nest: Bank Swallow, Cliff Swallow, Barn Swallow, Tree Swallow (in holes), etc. Some nest in colonies, some alone--Tree Swallows may nest in bluebird boxes; Purple Martins may nest in "martin houses" if the surroundings are suitable.

BARN SWALLOW

Some nest in holes, and some "glue" their nests to the sides of buildings or natural structures using mud and their glutinous saliva.

Usually 4-7 eggs are laid and incubation may be 13-16 days. The young usually leave the nest after 22-28 days, returning to the nest or nest site during the first days of freedom to be fed, then less and less often. Their food consists of moths, ants, beetles, butterflies, grasshoppers, spiders, dragonflies, small flies, leaf hoppers, etc. Feed insect-eating diet; supplement with insects as soon as possible. Tapping on the sides of their bills may stimulate them to gape. For raising and releasing, see **RELEASING** section in **ALTRICIAL BIRDS** chapter and **FLYING-INSECT-EATERS** and **SWIFT** sections.

TITMICE, NUTHATCHES, CHICKADEES

TUFTED TITMOUSE

BLACK-CAPPED CHICKADEE

These birds tend to nest mostly in holes in trees, sometimes in nest boxes. Nests have 4-8 eggs per nest and incubation is about 12 days. When 6 days old, the young have their eyes open and rows of pin-feather shafts can be seen among the body down. The young leave the nest when about 16 days old. Their food consists of insects (butterflies and moths and their eggs, larvae, and pupae, beetles, wood borers, leaf hoppers, small tent caterpillars, wasps, plant lice and their eggs), seeds, fruit (blueberries, raspberries, mulberries, bayberries, etc.). Feed seed-eater diet and make the formula very mushy and pureed. Small seed-eaters get impacted crops if their formula is lumpy! These birds may take more time to learn to eat on their own. Be patient!

For feeding and releasing, see **FEEDING** and **RELEASING** sections in **GENERAL CARE OF ORPHANED BIRDS** and **ALTRICIAL BIRDS** chapters.

OTHER INSECT-EATING BIRDS

VIREOS   (see Swallows)

SHRIKES   (see Blue Jays and Hawks) grasshoppers, small birds, and mice

WRENS   (see Swallows) note: Wrens need to be fed every 5-10 minutes when very young, every 10-20 minutes thereafter.

TANAGERS   (see Flycatchers) also tent caterpillars and fruits

CUCKOOS   (see Flycatchers) also tent caterpillars and fruits

CREEPERS   (see Swallows) insects in tree bark

NOTE--These birds will not readily feed from a dish and may have to be hand-fed until released. Putting food in their cage to attract insects helps them to learn to feed on their own, but they generally will not get enough with this method to sustain themselves independent from formula. One enterprising person placed a young nighthawk on her arm outside in the evening and let mosquitoes bite her near the bird. When it was eating these on its own after several days, she released it.

WOODPECKERS (INCLUDING SAPSUCKERS AND FLICKERS)

RED-HEADED WOODPECKER

Generally, these are hole-nesting species (trees, posts, boxes). Four to 8 eggs may be laid at the bottom of a cavity, sometimes on a small bed of wood chips. Incubation may be from 12-14 days and the young are hatched naked and blind. Juvenal plumage is acquired before the young leave the nest, usually at about 3 weeks of age. They learn to climb at an early age. Food consists of insects, berries, acorns, sap, larvae of wood borers and beetles, adult beetles, grubs, ants, caterpillars, cocoons, blackberries, raspberries, dogwood berries, elderberries, grapes, cherries, apples, crickets, grasshoppers, and corn. Feed insect-eating diet and transfer to natural foods as soon as possible.

They usually feed by clinging to tree trunks and large branches. Place branches with rough bark in a cage so they may use them to crack seeds or look for food. Some, however, feed on the ground (flicker) or even in the air (Red-headed Woodpecker). These birds may come back for food for a longer period after being released. For feeding and releasing, see **FEEDING** and **RELEASING** sections in **GENERAL CARE OF ORPHANED BIRDS** and **ALTRICIAL BIRDS** chapters.

CEDAR WAXWINGS, MOCKINGBIRDS, THRASHERS, ORIOLES

Feed these birds the same diet as **WOODPECKERS**, but utilize lots of fruit.

For releasing, see **RELEASING** in **THRUSHES** section.

GULLS, TERNS
(precocial, but fed and housed as altricial)

Gulls and terns breed in colonies where nests are frequently placed on the ground amid sand and rocks or on rocky, craggy coastlines. Nests are often only 1-2 feet apart. Two to 4 eggs are laid and incubation is approximately 21 days.

HERRING GULL

The young remain in the nest for a few days but at 3-4 days of age are running about and hiding under rocks or vegetation.

They learn to swim at an early age, but are fed by the parents until fully grown and able to fish for themselves. When hatched, the young are covered with grayish, white, or tan down which camouflages them. Gulls frequently eat worms, grubs, and grasshoppers, but mostly small fish; therefore, feed them the insect-eater diet plus small fish. Transfer them to small fish and insects as soon as possible. Food for terns is most commonly small fish and aquatic mollusks. For feeding, see **FEEDING** section in **HERONS, CRANES, AND BITTERNS** chapter. Release near a large body of open water following **RELEASING** section in **HERONS, CRANES, AND BITTERNS** chapter.

NIGHTHAWKS, WHIP-POOR-WILLS
(precocial, but fed and housed as altricial)

These birds have poorly developed feet and spend most of their time in the air or squatting horizontally on a wide limb or flat surface--on the ground or roof-top, where they nest. Nighthawks may nest downtown and can be heard above the city in the evening "peenting" as they search for insects.

Usually only 2 eggs are laid per nest site--generally building no nest but laying the eggs in a shallow depression, depending upon camouflage to conceal them. Incubation is about 15-20 days and the hatchlings are covered with a soft down with a color pattern which provides camouflage in their natural environment. By 13-15 days, the down begins to be replaced by a juvenal plumage. The young can run about soon after hatching, but are fed by the adults until they can fly. Food consists of moths, butterflies, grasshoppers, crickets, mosquitoes, beetles, flies, flying ants, and ants. Up to 50 species of insects have been found in the stomachs of these birds. One bird's stomach contained 2,173 ants, others over 500 mosquitoes! Feed insect-eater's diet and supplement with small chunks of beef liver and insects.

These birds do not seem to need a long release period--readily catching insects as soon as they can fly well. Placing a light bulb in their cage and turning it on at night helps attract moths and other insects so that the birds can learn to feed on natural food while being fed the food formula. For releasing, see **RELEASING** section in **ALTRICIAL BIRDS** chapter and **SWIFT** section.

BLUE JAYS, CROWS, RAVENS, STARLINGS

COMMON GRACKLE

AMERICAN CROW

Nests are placed in pine or deciduous trees where, at times, they may be added to, growing in size from year to year--1 European Starling nest measured almost 2' long. Blue Jay nests are smaller, perhaps 7-8" wide. Four to 7 eggs are usually laid per clutch and incubation lasts about 17-18 days. The young open their eyes at 5-6 days of age. Their diet is highly varied; being omnivorous, they eat anything digestible: insects, seeds, fruits, parts of amphibians and reptiles, small mice, snails, eggs, and grains. Feed insecteater diet and transfer gradually to their natural food as soon as possible. The natural habitat is varied--woods and fields primarily.

For feeding and releasing, see **FEEDING** and **RELEASING** sections in **GENERAL CARE OF ORPHANED BIRDS** and **ALTRICIAL BIRD** chapters.

SEED-EATERS

SPARROWS, CARDINALS, GROSBEAKS, GOLDFINCHES, TOWHEE, JUNCOS, LARKS, MEADOWLARKS, GRACKLES, OTHER BLACKBIRDS

All of these feed on seeds, insects, and fruit. (Meadowlarks may consume more insects than the others do; however, they may all be fed the same diet.) All nest in a variety of habitats, but some are more specific to certain habitats than others: grackles prefer pine trees; Red-winged Blackbirds prefer marshes or thickets; meadowlarks nest on the ground or in thick grasses in open fields. All young birds can grasp, gape, swallow, and defecate

CARDINAL

by "uncoordinated wigglings." Their eyes may open at 3-5 days and the young may leave the nest at 14-21 days, depending upon the species.

Feed seed-eater diet (mealworms may be added) and transfer to a natural diet of seeds, grains, and insects as soon as possible. Add grit to formula when the eyes are open and birds begin pecking on the cage bottom. The bills of seed-eating birds are larger, thicker, and shorter than those of insect-eating birds. For feeding and releasing, see **FEEDING** and **RELEASING** sections in **ALTRICIAL BIRDS** chapter.

DOVES, PIGEONS

Doves and pigeons may nest singly or in small colonies. The males collect the nest materials and bring them to the females who build the somewhat flimsy nests. The nest is loose and shallow, made of

MOURNING DOVE

sticks, twigs, and finer vegetation. Two broods may be raised in 1 season. Almost always 2 eggs are laid per clutch and the incubation period is 14-16 days. The adults take turns incubating the white eggs. The young, sometimes referred to as "squab," are hatched helpless and thinly covered with short, white down. Juvenal plumage and quills appear shortly, perhaps within 4-7 days. Young are fed regurgitated food known as "pigeon milk" or "dove milk." This is a cheesey fluid high in protein and fat and somewhat similar to rabbit's milk. After a few days this is supplemented with partially digested grains. By the time the young leave the nest at 2-3 weeks, they are fed mostly whole grains. Young in the wild take the food directly from the parents' crops--inserting their bills into their parents' mouths to receive the semi-liquid pap. After leaving the nest the young are fed for about a week by the adults. Many, but not all, doves migrate south for the winter.

WHAT TO DO FIRST
See **WHAT TO DO FIRST** section in **ALTRICIAL BIRDS** chapter.

HOUSING
See **HOUSING** section in **ALTRICIAL BIRDS** chapter.

FEEDING
Use 8-in-1 Mynah Bird Food or chick starter ground in a blender and moistened until thick and soupy. To 2 tbs. Mynah Bird Food or chick starter add 1 tbs.

high protein baby cereal, 1 tbs. wheat germ, 1 tbs. corn meal, 1 tsp. baby egg yolk, and 2 to 3 drops liquid vitamin. Mix with water to make a mush--cooked oatmeal or cream of wheat may be added. As birds mature, add seeds such as millet or parakeet seed to the formula.

Use an eyedropper with the end cut off (or an eyedropper without a pointed end) for easier flow of the birds' thick mush. Make certain all edges are **smooth** so you will not cut the throat or crop. Some volunteers prefer to use 1 cc tuberculin syringes for feeding. The birds will poke their heads around and open their mouths sporadically. Hold them so that you can insert a finger in the side of the bill to hold it open while you insert the dropper. Be sure to place the dropper beyond the glottis (hole in the middle of the lower bill) because this is the air passageway to the lungs. Then fill the crop--adding food until the crop feels like a slushy, plump pillow--not hard (usually 4 to 5 eyedroppers-full per feeding). Because these birds can hold a lot of food at a time, they need only be fed every 4-5 hours. Pigeons always will act hungry and squeak for food, but do not overfeed them. The crop should have some food in it always, but will "deflate" overnight.

As soon as birds begin to walk around, leave seeds (millet, parakeet seed, etc.) and unmedicated chick or duck mash on the bottom of the cage--they usually get curious and start pecking at the food. Once you are certain the bird is eating seeds, begin to decrease feedings over several days until the bird is eating on its own. Place grit (parakeet grit or fine gravel) in with seeds because birds need this to "chew" or grind the seeds in their gizzards. Natural foods include all types of whole grains and weed seeds.

RELEASE

As soon as the birds are eating well and are feathered (including tail feathers 2-3" long), place their cage outdoors for 5-7 days (see instructions for outdoor aviary)--then open the door; release and continue to feed them until they do not return for food for 5-7 days. Release should be made in an area where wild seeds are plentiful and when the weather forecast is good.

See **RELEASE** section in **ALTRICIAL BIRDS** chapter.

HERONS, CRANES, BITTERNS

GREAT BLUE HERON

These long-necked, long-legged birds spend much time wading along shores of lakes, streams, marshes, and other bodies of water looking for food. Their natural diet consists of frogs, small fishes, small rodents, amphibians, reptiles, insects, and most other small aquatic animals. Nesting occurs in late spring to early summer. Nests are made of sticks and leaves and are concealed along edges of wetland areas or built in trees. Great Blue Herons, common to our area, build large, flimsy nests in colonies (rookeries) high in trees. Green-backed Herons sometimes nest 10-20 feet off the ground singly or in small colonies. Nests generally contain 3-7 eggs and the incubation period is 17-28 days.

Young are awkward and ungainly and are covered with gray, white, or buff down. Juvenal plumage appears at 7-10 days of age. Birds may leave the nest for the first time as early as 2-3 weeks, although they cannot fly yet. Young may be fed in the wild anywhere from 1 or 2 times to 7 times in the morning and the same number in the afternoon. They are fed soft regurgitated food when very

YOUNG HERON

young--the adult sticking its bill down the throat of the young bird and placing the food in the crop. At about 2 weeks of age, the young receive small bits of whole food.

HOUSING

Keep young birds in a large, tall container (box or cage) with a light bulb for warmth until the birds are feathered (2-3 weeks maximum). Use newspapers or diapers on the bottom of the cage for easy cleaning and have a small flat container with a diaper or newspaper shreds for a "nest" to lie in. Clean the box after each feeding, but wait to see if the bird will keep food down first. When the birds are feathered and walking around, transfer them to an outdoor cage. Position the cage so one end is in a natural body of water. The cage should be of tight mesh material so that minnows can be placed in the submerged area of the cage and cannot escape. Perches should be added and a partial top and sides provided as shelter against rain.

FEEDING

Feed these birds live or very fresh minnows, crayfish, frogs, grasshoppers, or worms. Some people have raised herons on raw beef, earthworms, fresh herring, mice, and chopped freshly killed or thawed fish. Cod liver oil and balanced vitamins should be added regularly. Minnows may be caught by seining in lakes or may be purchased in bait shops or at fish hatcheries.

Touch the birds gently on the side of the bill with meat and then hold it in front so they can see what it looks like--hold a minnow by its tail with head evident. These birds usually stop eating when full (you may have to force-feed the first few times). Feed every 2 hours or so, or feed as their parents would, in the morning and evening. Provide 5-24 minnows per meal, depending upon appetite and size of fish. After the bird learns what the food looks like, put minnows or other live food in a clear dish of water in the cage. After a few days, the birds will learn to feed themselves completely and will no longer need to be fed by hand. Older birds may eat 40-50 1" minnows per meal from a glass dish with water.

RELEASE

Release the birds when the fuzz has begun disappearing from their heads and the birds fly well. Open the outdoor cage door and continue to place minnows in a glass dish outside the cage 2 times each day. Gradually the birds will wean themselves from the cage and its food and will learn to hunt on their own. Stop feeding only when food has been untouched for 4-5 days.

Make certain the outdoor cage is near or partially in water. Birds should be in an outdoor cage at least 2-3 weeks before release. Make sure the weather prediction is good for the next 3 days or so after releasing.

SPECIAL NOTE

Do **NOT** lean into or bend near the box containing a heron or bittern. These birds will stab at anything shiny, including eyes! When frightened or upset, wading birds will regurgitate food.

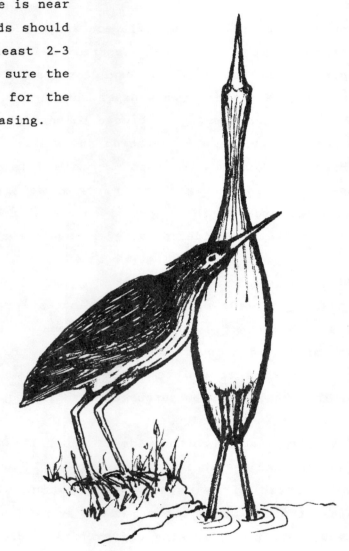

Heron and bittern leg care is very important. Clean their legs once a week with mild soap and put vaseline on them once a week if they are in an indoor facility.

GREEN HERON

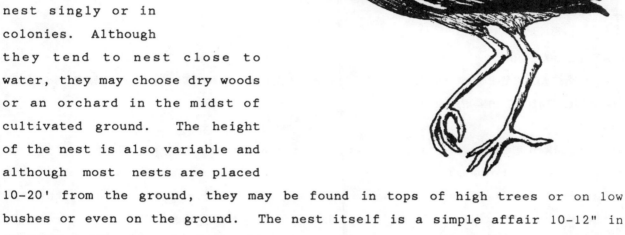

IN THE WILD

Green-backed Herons
nest singly or in
colonies. Although
they tend to nest close to
water, they may choose dry woods
or an orchard in the midst of
cultivated ground. The height
of the nest is also variable and
although most nests are placed
10-20' from the ground, they may be found in tops of high trees or on low
bushes or even on the ground. The nest itself is a simple affair 10-12" in
diameter, ill-adapted, it would seem, to hold eggs when the tree branches
wave in the wind. It is merely a flat platform of sticks, destitute of any
sort of lining and not cup-shaped. The nest is so thin and flimsy that one
can sometimes look through it from below and see the eggs.

Green-backed Herons may lay 3-9 eggs but the ordinary clutch consists of 4-5
eggs. The incubation period is 17 days. The young at an early age are expert
climbers among the branches of the nesting tree long before they are able to
fly. In climbing they make use of their feet, wings, and bill or neck,
hooking their bills and chins over the branches and pulling themselves up.
It may be the less-than-expert climbers that are brought to our
rehabilitation programs.

When first hatched, the herons stretch to a height of almost 4" and when a
week old they are 11". The young gain about 1/2 ounce a day, weighing
almost an ounce when born and almost 4 ounces in a week. The young are
normally fed in the early morning and in the late afternoon, the greatest
activity being 4-6 A.M. and 5-7 P.M. One observer recorded that the young
were fed 7 times in the morning and 7 times in the evening. The food is
primarily regurgitated, but not predigested, small fish.

125

The food of the Green-backed Heron varies somewhat with the locality. In birds taken in fresh-water habitats, the stomach contents consist of tadpoles, water insects and their larvae, crayfish, and small fish. Food is also gathered in the uplands by these birds and their stomachs have been found to contain earthworms, crickets, grasshoppers, snakes, and other small animals. They are day-feeders and prefer the early morning and late afternoon.

WHAT TO DO FIRST

See **GENERAL CARE OF ORPHANED BIRDS** chapter and **WHAT TO DO FIRST** section in **ALTRICIAL BIRDS** chapter.

Green-backed Herons are expert fishers at a very young age. Keeping that in mind, when herons are received in a program, and are uninjured and otherwise healthy, place them in a cage with a clear glass dish with live minnows. Leave them in a quiet place for several hours. When you return, you will discover either that they can feed themselves or that you need to begin a regime of hand-feeding.

Keep young, downy birds in cages with multiple perches and supplemental warmth from lights. If they are not self-feeders, feed them live minnows 4 times daily. They will refuse the fish when their crops are full. Always provide them with a dish with fresh live minnows so when they are able to self-feed, the fish will be there.

PRECAUTIONS

Herons are easily alarmed and will regurgitate their meal on the slightest provocation. It is therefore a good policy to enter their presence only to feed them and clean their cage. A Green-backed Heron at any age will stab its long, sharp bill at anything shiny. This includes rings, watches, and eyes. So, either wear protective eye-gear or make sure you have a grip on the bird's neck when feeding.

Green-backed Herons are usually self-feeders by 3 weeks and flying well and ready to be released by 4-5 weeks. The Green-backed Heron release cages should be placed on the shore of the release-site lake. The cage should be placed about 1/3 in the water and 2/3 on the shore. Place live minnows plus

crayfish, frogs, and tadpoles in a large container that also contains
appropriate natural items such as rocks, logs, etc. The cage size will vary
with the number of birds housed.

When the herons are of release age and have acquired appropriate size and
flying skills, they can be released. Wait for release until good weather is
predicted for 3-4 days. Place the fish pool outside the cage and continue
to stock it with minnows. Herons will continue to return to the release site
for fish for about 5 days. They will eat fewer and fewer fish until they
return to the site but don't eat the fish.

When release pens are away from human habitation and located on lake shores,
any outside release cage must be completely predator-proof.

BELTED KINGFISHER

BELTED KINGFISHER

IN THE WILD

As a species the Belted Kingfisher covers nearly all of North America. Essentially a fish-eating bird, its major habitat is near large or small bodies of water.

The nest of the kingfisher is in a burrow in a sandy, clay, or gravelly bank. The chosen site is usually near water and near the bird's favorite fishing sites. The burrow extends inward, sloping slightly upward for varying distances, usually 3-6' but sometimes as much as 10' or even 15'. The nest is placed in an enlarged chamber which may be directly at the end of the tunnel or a little to one side of it. The chamber varies considerably in size and shape but is approximately circular and dome-shaped. It is usually 10-12" in diameter and 6-7" high. Often the eggs are laid on the bare sand or gravel but usually the nesting chamber is lined with bits of clean fish bone or leaves and grasses.

The number of eggs laid by the kingfisher varies from 5 to 8, the commonest number being 6. Only 1 brood is raised in a season. The eggs are short-ovate, smooth and glossy, and pure white in color.

The incubation period is 23-24 days in length. The young remain in the nest for about 4 weeks and do not leave the nest until they are able to fly. The young keep warm by covering each other with their wings. The parent bird feeds the young with regurgitated, but not pre-digested, fish.

Once they have fledged, the mother must teach her young to fish. A mother has been observed to catch a fish, beat it to death and then drop the dead fish in the water for the young to retrieve. She continues this and after a few days begins dropping live minnows for her young to catch. It usually takes the mother 10 days to complete the training.

The young kingfishers are hatched naked, blind, and helpless; with a huge conical bill. The eyes open at about 2 weeks. Within a week or less the pinfeathers or feather-sheaths appear. When the young birds are 17-18 days old, the sheaths rapidly burst and the juvenal plumage appears. In this plumage, the young kingfishers look strikingly like the adult.

The kingfishers are fish-eaters and would probably live on fish exclusively if they were always able to secure all they needed. They catch mainly small fish, preferably not over 6" long. The kingfishers must of necessity do their fishing in clear water so they seldom are seen on muddy streams or ponds or on those that are choked or overgrown with thick vegetation. They usually perch on a stake, snag, or pier standing in the water or on some bare, overhanging branch where they can watch for fish. From such a perch, the birds may dive obliquely into the water to seize the fish in their powerful bills. Or they may rise 30-40' into the air, hover for a few seconds and then disappear beneath the water for several seconds. When fish are not readily obtainable, the kingfishers may make use of various other kinds of food--crabs, crayfish, frogs, snakes, beetles, and even berries. Some have been reported eating butterflies and small precocial birds.

HOUSING

Housing for non-flying kingfishers can be supplied by a round container filled with soft nesting materials covered with a box to resemble the cavity housing of the kingfisher in the wild. This container then is put inside a larger cage. The kingfishers rarely venture outside their nesting container and keep each other warm by covering each other with their wings. If the birds aren't feathered, use supplemental heating sources.

See **HOUSING** section in **ALTRICIAL BIRDS** chapter.

FEEDING

Kingfishers need to be force-fed live minnows 4 times a day. Feed birds until their crops are full, but not bulging. Normally these birds will refuse fish when they are full and will regurgitate all you have fed them if you try to force more into them. They will also regurgitate the contents of their crop if startled or frightened. It is therefore not wise to interact with these birds in any way except to feed them and clean the cage. Seine for minnows daily--keeping only the fish about 2" in length. Throw back any sport fish that are netted.

Feed the kingfishers by gently applying pressure at the corners of the bill to open the mouth and then insert the minnow head first. It is important to be sure the minnow goes past the bird's air vent and into the crop.

RELEASE

When the birds begin to fly, house them in release/flight cages. Cages should be equipped with multiple perches of varying heights, nesting boxes, and a large pool in which live minnows are placed. Allow the birds at least 5 hours to adapt to their new surroundings before attempting to enter the cage and feed them.

Kingfishers don't seem to fish instinctively and must be taught to recognize their food source and also how to catch the fish. When the kingfishers are 3-4 weeks old and are flying well, begin the process of teaching them to fish.

To teach the birds to fish, enter the cage and sit quietly until the birds seem calm. Catch a minnow out of the pool with long tweezers. Offer the fish to the bird and, when it starts to take the fish, drop the fish back into the water. Continue doing this for each bird for about 10 fish. If this doesn't stimulate the birds to take the fish from the water, begin the same process using dead fish. The dead minnow is offered to the bird, then dropped near it. The birds will usually pick the dead fish out of the water and eat them before they will attempt to catch live fish. It usually takes about 3 days of this teaching before the birds begin to take the fish from the pool themselves. During this time, continue hand-feeding the birds until they are securing an adequate diet themselves. Determine this by checking the number of fish in the pool and by checking the crops of the individual birds.

When the kingfishers are successfully fishing, they should be released. The birds should be released either in the area where they were originally found or in the area where the release caging was located.

HAWKS AND OWLS

Because raptors are protected by both state and federal law, these birds are not sent home with volunteers but are raised and released at the Center.

IN THE WILD

Hawks and owls are predators, meaning they take and kill other animals for food. They are a valuable and necessary part of the ecological food chain, keeping within a normal, healthy balance the numbers of small animals by removing the old, sick, unwary, and diseased individuals from breeding populations. Their diet consists of mice, voles, rabbits, opossums, skunks, rats, squirrels, fish,

EASTERN SCREECH-OWLS

insects, reptiles, amphibians, and various species of birds. Most larger hawks and owls begin establishing territories and mating in the late fall and nest in January and February, while snow is still on the ground. The average clutch size is 1-3 eggs. Smaller hawks (American Kestrel) and Eastern Screech-Owls nest somewhat later and are hatched in April or May. Hawks and owls raise only 1 brood per year.

Incubation for large raptors is normally 3-4 weeks and the young hatch 1-2 days apart, remaining in the nest 4-5 weeks. They are covered with soft, white, cream, or gray down when hatched and begin to be active and walk around the nest in 5-10 days. Eyes begin to focus around 10 days. Wing quills sprout at about 14-17 days and full adult feathers are acquired by about 4 weeks of age when the last of the down on the head starts to disappear. Young usually fledge from the nest onto the ground at about 4-5 weeks, managing to find cover or to get themselves up into the lower branches of nearby trees where the adults continue to feed them until they are ready to fly and learn to develop their own hunting skills. Often this takes up to 3 months, especially for the larger raptors. Hawks feed and are more active by day, owls by night. They may live in the same habitats, but are active at different times.

Always try to raise 2 or more young of the same species together. See **IMPRINTING** chapter.

WHAT TO DO FIRST
When a raptor comes to you, examine it carefully for injuries (wounds, broken bones, etc.) to determine its condition. If healthy and warm, proceed with housing and feeding. If injured, see first aid section or call a vet. If cold, weak, and dehydrated, warm the animal first--you can kill a bird by feeding it when it is cold or it can die from the cold. To warm the bird: cup it in your hands; put it against your body and hold it; place it in the nest box or bowl; cover it lightly and place it near a light bulb or on a heating pad turned down low with towels between the pad and the bird.

Unfeathered birds (1 week or younger) should be kept at a temperature of 80-90°F. Downy birds with a few quills showing can be kept at 80-85°F. Birds with feather quills and small feathers can be kept at 75-80°F. Fully feathered birds can be kept at room temperature.

If the bird can lift its head and is active after warming, feed it mixtures listed in the section on **FEEDING** for hawks and owls in this chapter. If the bird is weak and dehydrated, **carefully** place 2-4 drops of re-hydrating solution into the throat **beyond the breathing hole at the base of the** tongue every 1/4 hour for the first 1-2 hours. When the bird begins to revive, feed it small pieces of beef or beef heart every 2 hours or so. For emaciated hawks and owls (those which lack the muscle tissue around the breast bone-keel) continue feeding re-hydration solution and Nutrical for 10-20 hours to get energy into the bird so that it will not die using its last energy resources trying to digest food. When the bird recovers strength and is healthy, feed it very 6 hours or 3-4 times per day.

HOUSING

Use a large box or cage with a 60-watt light bulb placed at an adequate distance for proper warmth. If the bird lies down often, shivers, or seems lethargic, it may be too cold. Healthy raptors do not need as much heat as other birds because they can maintain their own body temperatures better. Perches are needed as the birds get older; a log or branch at least the size of a human wrist is adequate. A small cardboard box lined with diapers or towels for support and warmth should be provided until the bird can walk. Baby raptors lie face down when they sleep. As the birds mature, the sides as well as the bottom of the box or cage should be lined with newspaper because raptors tend to "shoot" when they excrete wastes. As the young begin to focus their eyes and begin to move around, place small pieces of branches and sticks on the bottom of the box to simulate the nest and help coordination.

FEEDING

Young should be fed cut-up beef heart and beef liver dipped in bone meal (not the kind that you put on your garden, but the kind available in pet stores), balanced powdered or liquid vitamins, and occasionally as they get older, meat dipped in milk and wrapped in hair or fine cotton fiber. Small pieces of mice, rabbits, etc., may be fed. After 10-12 days of age raptors seem to need some hair or other roughage to help control the amount of secretion in their crops for digesting food.

To get the birds to eat, tap the sides of their beaks with the food; but if the birds do not open their beaks, you may have to force-feed them for the first few times by gently prying their beaks open and pressing the food to the back of the mouth. Feed 4-6 pieces per feeding. Eventually the birds will learn to take the food on their own. When they begin to get their feather sheaths, try dropping the food from your hand to the floor and leaving it there. The birds will learn to pick it up and tear it apart on their own as they mature.

Continue to hand-feed until you are certain that the birds are picking up enough food on their own to sustain themselves. Gradually increase the size of meat pieces until the entire mouse or other prey may be given. Learn the food call of the young and make a similar sound when you are feeding. If possible, obtain the feathered skin of an adult of the same species and place it over your hand as you feed to help the young birds associate food-giving with their own kind instead of with human hands.

As your raptors mature, be careful to avoid their talons when you clean or feed them. The beak may hurt if you are bitten, but the talons are powerful weapons and can cause puncture wounds or scratches.

RELEASING

As soon as most of the adult feathers emerge, place raptors outdoors in a cage large enough for them to fly, so that they may develop their flight muscles. Cage width should be 4 times wider than the width of the bird's wings outstretched. Cages should also be 15-30 feet long with rope-wrapped perches and areas sheltered from the weather. Place in the cage a pan of fresh water for bathing (to get rid of lice and mites) and a feeding platform which the birds can identify with food. Also, periodically scatter grain on the floor or ground inside the cage to attract small rodents for "hunting practice" and for learning to identify wild food.

ROUGH-LEGGED HAWK

Try to place as much natural food as you can locate in the cage. **Fresh** road kills can be a good source. The Nature Center has a source of freshly killed rats and mice which are frozen and used as needed. Raptors are fed 5-8 mice each per day. One day a week should be a fast day (no food).

The Nature Center generally tries to release young raptors in July or August of the year they were hatched. They are banded before release and the door of the release pen is opened after wild young have come off their nests, so that the wild adults will no longer be territorial and will be less likely to drive an "intruder" out of their territory. The feeding station is placed outside the pen and fresh mice are left daily. After release, it may take the raptors a few days to relocate the food supply, so don't stop feeding. It takes 2-3 months for these birds to learn to hunt on their own skillfully enough to survive. Keep feeding them until they have not returned for 2 weeks--they will come less and less frequently and finally not at all. Occasionally, in **hard** winters, we re-institute the feeding station in case the birds may return. Release only when good weather forecast for the next few days and release in a wild natural area, not in an urban or suburban area.

Do not put a predator near a cage housing any prey animal. Try not to put a hawk and owl in the same cage or in cages next to each other. Do not put different species of hawks together or different species of owls together.

Make sure the birds have killed their own prey for at least a week before releasing them.

PRECOCIAL BIRDS

Precocial birds are covered with feather down, can see, walk or swim, and feed themselves a few minutes or hours after hatching. They are not confined to the nest for long. Ducks, geese, pheasants, quail, killdeer, woodcock, and other shorebirds are precocial birds. Some precocial birds are housed and fed in the same manner as altricial birds--see that section.

MALLARD
DUCKLINGS

JUVENILE MALLARD
OR FEMALE

MALE MALLARD

IN THE WILD

Waterfowl spend nearly all their lives in or near water, nesting, breeding, and feeding on or near wet areas. Nesting may take place from April to July and most clutch sizes are 5-16 eggs, laid 1 per day. The female usually builds the nest and lines it with vegetation and with down from her breast. Incubation is usually 27-34 days, depending on the species. As soon as the young are dry from hatching, in 12-25 hours, they are led to water, which may be a few yards or a mile away from the nest. At about 3 weeks of age, the young begin to lose their downy feathers and are fully feathered and able to fly when 50-70 days old.

Wild food includes bulrushes, pond weeds, millet, smartweed and other aquatic plants, grasses, leaves and blossoms of clover, mollusks, small fish, alfalfa, soybeans, peas, rice, and many cultivated grains such as corn, wheat, barley, and oats.

Most waterfowl migrate south for the winter.

BOBWHITE

PHEASANTS, QUAIL, AND GROUSE are birds of woodlots and fields and cleverly conceal their nests in thick vegetation--the birds appearing to blend perfectly into their surroundings.

Nests are made of dead grasses and soft vegetation. Usually 6-15 eggs are laid and incubation is 20-24 days. As soon as the down on the chicks has dried, the adult leads them in search of food. Weight gain is slow during the first week.

Quail obtain some adult wing feathers early and can fly when a week old. "Wild" food includes insects, weed seeds, acorns, fruits, berries, some cultivated grain crops, spiders, and some mollusks--feeding in early morning and early evening.

KILLDEER, WOODCOCK, SNIPE, and other shorebirds live and nest in a variety of habitats from woods to fields to marshes. Most species do not select habitats as wet as those of wading birds. Woodcock and snipe nests are well camouflaged in leaves and grasses. The adult incubating or brooding the nest is flushed out only with great difficulty. Killdeer and other shorebirds generally prefer to nest near wet areas, although some Killdeer nests have been found in fields and gravel pits and on roof-tops.

KILLDEER

These shorebird nests and eggs are generally on the ground in the open, but so well camouflaged that only rarely are they found. Usually 4 eggs are laid and incubation may be 21-26 days. The adults usually remove all bits of shell from the nest immediately after hatching, and, as soon as they are dry, the downy young run along after the adults searching for food. They "bob" and call at an early age. Both parents employ the wounded-wing act, often drawing predators away from the nest or young.

Woodcocks feed largely on earthworms. Killdeer and other shorebirds which frequent a variety of habitats, consume large quantities of insects, such as grasshoppers, crickets, locusts, beetles, caterpillars, flies, and ants. Those shorebirds which feed largely in or near water consume aquatic insects, insect larvae, small crustaceans, worms, and aquatic seeds.

WHAT TO DO FIRST

Follow procedure in **GENERAL CARE OF ORPHANED BIRDS** chapter. When the bird comes to you, examine it carefully to determine its condition. If **healthy** and **warm**, proceed with housing and feeding.

If injured, consult a supervisor or call a vet. If cold, weak, and dehydrated, warm the animal first--you can kill it by feeding it when it is cold. To warm the bird: cup it in your hands; put it against your body and hold it; place it in the nest box or bowl; or cover it lightly and place it near a light bulb or on a heating pad turned down low, with towels between the pad and the bird. Newborn birds (1 week or younger) should be kept at a temperature of 85-90°F. Downy birds with a few quills showing can be kept at 80-85°F. Birds with feather quills and small feathers can be kept at room temperature.

If the bird can lift its head and is active after warming, feed it mixtures listed below. If the bird is weak and dehydrated, **carefully** place 2-4 drops of re-hydration solution into the throat **beyond the breathing hole at the base of the tongue** every 1/4 hour for the first 1-2 hours. When the bird begins to revive a little, feed it formula every 30-45 minutes. You may have to force-feed a precocial bird if it is weak.

Birds do not need to be fed at night unless they are very weak.

HOUSING

A large box with a light bulb will suffice and the bottom may be lined with newspapers or diapers. Arrange the heat and light so that the chicks have a warm spot in the box and a cool spot in case they

LIGHT FIXTURE

need to get away from the heat. Hang a feather duster in the box so the young may run under it. The duster simulates the parent bird and thus provides support, comfort, and shelter. Young chicks may run around and peep themselves to death if they do not have an arrangement such as this. A screen should be placed over the top of the box because some young can jump rather high, especially as they get older and try their wings.

These birds thrive on quiet and as little disturbance as possible. Place the box in an area of the house where the **only** disturbance they will receive is when someone changes the food or cleans the cage. Placing cut-up bits of fresh green grass and clover or colored objects in or near the food dish may help them learn to peck more readily--large marbles work well. Do not put water in this box other than water in an inverted mason jar. See illustration.

FEEDING

A large mason jar with a feeding lid or a small chicken or turkey feeder (available from a farm store) makes a good feeding dish. Be sure the lid is small enough that the bird cannot get into the water. Unmedicated turkey starter, duck mash, or chicken starter, with wheat germ and boiled egg yolk or baby egg yolk are nutritious, well-balanced diets. Sprinkle the food mixture around the floor of the box and place some in the feed dish. The feed dish will contain a jar in the middle with water, upside down so that small amounts seep into the lid or small feeder; the bird then has a choice of dry food, moist food, or plain or slurry water. Change the food supply 1-2 times a day and, as the young grow, add insects, worms, grains, and berries to their food mixture. Add 6-7 drops of balanced vitamins with B-12 drops daily to the mixture. Do not place any other water in the box.

RELEASING

When birds show signs of flying and are getting their adult feathers (about 1 month of age), place them in an outside flight pen which is long enough to allow them to fly around. The top should be covered with solid wood or a tarp to protect against severe weather. Feed them their natural foods by using a tub with duck weed (for waterfowl); by sprinkling natural grains and sugar on the bottom of the cage to attract insects for Killdeer and shore birds; and by supplying turkey, duck, or chicken starter mixture with cracked corn over the bottom of the cage for all. Woodcock need deep soil with worms and insects. Ducks also need greens and soil regularly. If ducks that are still downy get messy, they may swim for short periods of time in a shallow tub of fresh water, but should be blown dry with a hair dryer set on low, if they are very young, so that they do not get chilled. Young ducks should not be left in water very long because they get tired swimming and may drown. Keep birds in outdoor cages for 2 weeks or more before releasing them. Birds should be fully feathered, flying, and eating on their own at release. They should have water-proof feathers. Do not keep them too long, however, because they need time to survive on their own before fall migration time arrives. Release precocial birds in their natural habitats--pheasants in fields, ducks in marshes or lakes, Killdeer on river banks near open fields (especially gravelly ones), Woodcock near marshes or streams, and other shorebirds near mud flats or beaches.

TIPS FROM ANIMAL CARE VOLUNTEERS

Some volunteers prefer a light bulb to a heating pad because they think the heat can "flow" down and around the young. Make certain the feed dish with the water jar is the small size. Wet, chilled baby ducks die easily.

Dust all game birds (grouse, pheasants) with cat flea powder once a week to prevent outbreaks of mites and lice--sprinkle powder on your hands then rub into birds' feathers--avoiding eyes. Do this until the light is removed as a heat source.

Precocial birds learn to eat by imitating parents. By cueing into natural sounds and natural sights, volunteers fabricate feeding situations for young Woodcock. Young respond to tapping sounds foraging adults make. Live worms are placed on the soil floor (changed daily) of the housing box. By tapping a shish kebab skewer near the worms (and flipping them slightly), the young can be stimulated to seek worms. Also, by loosely looping worms around a skewer (about 4" from tip) and tapping the soil near the young, the bird may take the worm off the skewer--as if from an adult's bill.

Wood Ducks are very flighty and will exhaust themselves trying to jump out of the box. It is essential that they be placed in a totally quiet area and disturbed only to change food and clean the cage.

One tip that has worked to get Wood Ducks to feed is to drop them from 3-4' above a water dish into the water. This action starts their feeding reflex. Be certain to dry off the ducks so they don't get chilled.

Mallards easily become tame if around humans too much. Put Mallards in an isolated, yet protected, area. Release them away from humans--they tend to swim up to people and can be harmed by motor boats, dogs, children, etc.

Do not mix species or different ages of the same species together. Often the younger or newer birds are killed by larger or stronger ones.

Identifying ducklings is often confusing. The illustrations below attempt to depict the differences between baby Mallards and baby Wood Ducks. The most obvious difference is in the eye stripe. Generally, the eye stripe on Mallards begins at the back of the head and continues through the eye down to the base of the upper bill. The stripe on the Wood Duck begins at the back of the head and stops at the eye. Coloration of the young of each species varies; but, generally, Wood Ducks are a paler yellow than Mallards. Although they may behave similarly when excited, on the whole, Wood Ducks are more easily alarmed and will remain jumpy for a longer period of time.

YOUNG MALLARD   YOUNG WOOD DUCK

REPTILES

GENERAL INFORMATION

Although native Michigan reptiles are rarely brought to the Kalamazoo Nature Center, and, therefore, the following information generally is not used here, it has been helpful to Nature Center staff in maintaining various reptiles for display and for caring for non-native forms brought to the Center.

Most reptiles are basically carnivorous, although some vary the diet with vegetation. Finding out what each species feeds on in the wild will help insure successful feeding in captivity.

Natural prey of snakes in the wild includes amphibians, birds and their eggs, mammals, other reptiles, fishes, and invertebrates. Whenever possible, snakes should be given the opportunity to capture their food alive. However, it is not always possible to maintain a live-animal-food supply. Snakes may be taught to eat thawed food at room temperature. Worm or fish slime rubbed on the fur of rodents entices primarily worm- or fish-eating snakes to eat rodents. It is easiest to teach snakes to eat thawed food if the food resembles prey the snakes normally capture in the wild.

The following basic diets for snakes have been used. Garter and water snakes prefer fish, frogs, earthworms, slugs, and toads. Rat Snakes, Boa Constrictors, Bull Snakes, and vipers should have rodents or birds of a size normally consumed in the wild. Brown or Ring-necked Snakes and their relatives will eat earthworms and small snakes, lizards, and salamanders. Lizards form the basic diet for racers and vine snakes; they can be given small rodents, also.

Lizards eat meat or vegetable matter, depending on the species. All lizards and other reptiles must have a proper calcium ratio in their diets. Most traditional diets are deficient in calcium. Supplementation with bone meal or crushed egg shells, or a diet primarily based on dog food, baby chicks, or mice will usually provide ample calcium. Horned Lizards ("Toads") prefer ants, but may be induced to eat crickets or meal worms. Worm Lizards (also known as Night Lizards) prefer ant eggs and termites.

Green Iguanas have been raised successfully on meal worms, thawed vegetables, baby mice, crickets, some moistened dog food, and dandelion flowers or leaves.

Turtles and tortoises are both carnivorous and herbivorous. Tortoises (prefer land) eat a balanced diet of fresh fruit, mushrooms, fresh greens, flowers, moistened dog food, and thawed frozen vegetables. Tortoises receive the major part of their liquid in their diet from the food they eat. Turtles (prefer water) eat earthworms, small mice, small fish, fresh greens, and occasionally hamburger.

Most reptiles need a supply of fresh water; some will not drink at all. It is necessary to study the natural habits and habitats of each species to determine how to get water into the animal's system. Some reptiles will drink from a water dish; others will not. Some get their water through droplets given to them, and some must have the water sprayed on leaves so they can lap it up, as after a rain.

Housing requirements for each species of reptile should be patterned after its natural environments with appropriate temperatures, shelter, light and dark components, and earth materials.

CARE AND FEEDING OF SNAKES

BLACK RAT SNAKE

CAGE

An aquarium is the best and simplest cage to use. Make a wooden frame and stretch fine wire mesh over it for use as a top. Snakes will rub against exposed surfaces and, if the cage is wire or unsanded wood, they easily can damage their skin and expose themselves to infection. A variety of bedding material can be used, from dried pine needles to small pea gravel, sand, wood shavings, or newspaper, although pine needles and gravel are preferred because they don't hold moisture quite so much and provide an even surface for the snake. When you feed the snake, make sure that it does not get any of the bedding on the food and swallow the bedding because it could cause serious problems with the snake's health.

CAGE EQUIPMENT

The cage should have a water bowl large enough for the snake to soak in before shedding. A rock, with rough but not sharp edges, to rub against is helpful when the animal is shedding. Most snakes will use a climbing log, preferably a smooth one with 1 or 2 branches; and it will make a cage more attractive.

FEEDING

Be sure you know what your animal would eat in the wild. Those that eat amphibians probably will take goldfish when hungry enough. Mammals can be supplied easily with pet store supplies of mice, rats, gerbils, and guinea pigs. Remember, the size of your snake will dictate the size of the animal required to keep it well fed. It is easier to feed a large snake an average-sized guinea pig than to try to feed it several large mice.

Some of the easily raised small creatures can be used for food for immature or small species. Never feed a snake live mice, rats, gerbils, etc., unless it is used to eating live food. Many snakes have been bitten by live prey. If you do feed live prey, watch the snake until it has eaten.

If you are having problems getting food for your snake, cool its cage, thus reducing the animal's metabolism and decreasing its need for food.

HANDLING

Some snakes will tame fairly easily, while others will never be "content" being handled. Usually, the smaller the snake, the easier it is to tame. Always wear gloves when first handling an animal. It will give you more confidence and prevent any new holes in your skin. As the snake takes to handling, you can keep it out for longer periods and allow it more freedom of movement. Eventually, you should find that it simply will hold onto you rather than the other way around. Never make quick movements or sudden sounds around a snake because it may react--positively or negatively.

DISEASE

Check snakes regularly for both mites and mouth rot. Both may be treated with a solution of 50% warm water and 50% hydrogen peroxide or vinegar. Treat any infected area at least once a day, making sure that the animal does not swallow any of the solution.

If the snake is be bitten or scratched by its prey, clean the wound with peroxide and make sure its bedding and water are especially clean until the wound has healed.

ADDENDA

HOW DOES ONE HANDLE A SICK BOA CONSTRICTOR?

Answer: Carefully, caringly, and with lots of help! The Nature Center's Boa Constrictor, Bella, lived, it is thought, to be over 30 years of age, was about 8' long and was viewed by visitors to the Center for the 17 years that she was in residence.

One day Bella was observed in her display case lying on her back trying to breathe. Wild Animal Rehabilitation Program Co-director Pat Adams was asked to help figure out what was wrong. After lots of talking and some head shaking, the conclusion was tentatively reached that Bella probably had pneumonia. It was decided to take her to a Program veterinarian, Dr. William Gregg, at Forest Hills Clinic in Plainwell.

By this time it was 4 in the afternoon, so Mrs. Adams, 3 dogs due to have their rabies shots for licenses, 1 daughter, 1 squirrel with a dislocated foot, 1 Screech Owl with scorched feet (from roosting in a chimney), and 1 very sick Boa Constrictor arranged themselves in the car and drove urgently to Forest Hills.

At the Clinic, Dr. Gregg confirmed the diagnosis--pneumonia--and searched through a large, impressive-looking book to come up with the necessary remedies. Bella was given a shot of antibiotic (gentamicin sulfate), had her heart and lungs listened to, and was instructed to drink fluids, keep warm, and stay under a vaporizer several hours each day. Under Dr. Gregg's instructions, Rehabilitation Program co-directors Pat Adams and Vicki Johnson, and Vicki's husband, Don Johnson, a Kalamazoo pediatrician, shared the responsibility of Bella's care for the first 6 days.

It was a learning experience from beginning to end. The first step was setting up the vaporizer to loosen the congestion in Bella's lungs. Towels and sheets were brought out and hung over the backs of chairs and counters to create a "mist tent" to hold the vapor. The family heating pad was placed under her box to keep body temperature consistently warm. The vaporizer, complete with medicine, was then placed under the mist tent.

The Boa Constrictor was so weak that she could not hold her head up or change position, so the moisture had to fall on her in a way not to drench her but to provide enough moisture to loosen the fluid in the lungs. She was given 2 additional shots of gentamicin sulfate in the next 2 days.

The next step was to keep fluids going into her system regularly. Imagine trying to place an eyedropper of re-hydration solution down the throat of a giraffe with mouth clenched shut and you have some idea of the challenge with Bella. Vicki located a syringe that measured about 7" long.

The method that worked most successfully was to hold Bella's head in one hand so that about 1' of neck stretched in an unbroken line. Then the eyedropper of fluid was worked through her mouth and down her neck along 1 side so as to miss the lung opening, and the fluid was then released. If we didn't feel the eyedropper going along inside her neck, we knew we had missed, and had to start all over again. This had to be done about every 4 hours during daylight hours.

Because she was so weak, it also was necessary to force vitamins and food down Bella. This was accomplished once a day in the same way that giving fluids was done. After the first 6 days, Bella was turned over to Wild Animal Rehabilitation Volunteer Pixie Goodrich for continued treatment. Pixie cared for Bella for 3 weeks.

We are happy to report that Bella recovered and lived several more years at the Nature Center. Because she was an old snake, extra precautions were taken to help prevent her becoming susceptible to pneumonia again. She had a heating pad on warm under the rug in her display case, and she received vitamins and food once a week--until her death of old age.

The final reward, that of Bella well and strong again, made all the unusual things we had to do when she was sick well worth the effort. And all those involved learned a great deal about how to handle a sick Boa Constrictor!

Upon learning of our experiences with Bella, Dick Solomon from Noah's Ark Pet Shop gave us his special formula for force-feeding a Boa Constrictor:

> 1 package unflavored Knox gelatin
>
> 2 teaspoons basic pet vitamins
>
> 1/2 teaspoon bone meal
>
> 1/4 capsule of 250 ml tetracycline
>
> 1 teaspoon brewer's yeast
>
> Add enough water to make this mixture
> soupy and feed to a Boa Constrictor
> with a long eyedropper.

To encourage the snake to begin eating on its own again after an illness, put a freshly killed mouse in with the snake--to stimulate feeding. Always keep vitamin C solution in fresh water in the cage.

Although Boa Constrictors are not native to Michigan, it seems logical to us that the methods we used for force-feeding and for caring for Bella should be able to be extrapolated and used for native snakes of similar feeding habits and for snakes with similar health problems.

ANOTHER UNIQUE CHALLENGE

COYOTE

The story of the coyotes begins the Tuesday after Memorial Day weekend (1981), when the Wild Animal Care and Rehabilitation Program received a call from John Wagner of Wayne State University. He was trying to find a home for 10 coyote pups, rather than see them destroyed. The pups had been found on Fighting Island, between Detroit and Canada (administered by the Canadian government). Apparently, a pair of coyotes had become stranded on the island when the ice went out and had given birth to the litter whose "den" was in an old drain pipe. Canadian authorities did not want the coyotes on the island, fearing they might not all find enough food to survive.

Mr. Wagner had helped get the coyotes off the island and had contacted all zoos in Michigan, looking for a home for them. Through the zoo contacts, he heard about the Nature Center's Wild Animal Care and Rehabilitation Program. Working with other Rehabilitation volunteers, Pat Adams put together a plan for raising and releasing the coyotes, then told Mr. Wagner the Nature Center would accept responsibility for the animals.

The coyotes arrived at the Center in early June. Five of them went north to the Wildlife Recovery Association of Midland. The remaining 5 were kept in 2 secluded pens at the Center while they matured. The coyotes were fed high-protein dog food and mice as a base food. Fresh road kills and some deer meat supplemented their diet. They much preferred the mice and wild food. All were vaccinated for distemper.

Then Pat Adams and family drove them north to Bellaire to the summer home of Animal Care volunteer Pixie Goodrich and her husband, Bob. The Goodriches enthusiastically agreed to build a large cage in the woods on their property where the coyotes stayed for another 2 weeks. Pixie made arrangements with local conservation officers for release into the Jordan State Game Area, about 20 miles away. After release, she, along with local Department of Natural Resources officers, maintained a food supply for them during the 2-3 weeks that it took for the young coyotes to develop hunting skills proficient enough to survive on their own.

It took all morning to capture the coyotes, load them into the transport cages and get them into the secluded release area. When the door to the cage was opened for them to go free, they shot out so fast that a camera shutter set at 1/25 second could not get a good photo of them. Follow-up reports indicated that they did return to the release site for food for about 3 weeks. The fact that they remained very wild in captivity and had a successful release makes for a happy ending.

The coyotes were released in northern Michigan because that is where Michigan's coyote population is naturally distributed and, therefore, chances for survival appeared to be greatest.

HOW WE OPERATE OUR PROGRAM

The Nature Center has been asked on many occasions and through many letters from people around the country to describe how the   Wild Animal Rehabilitation Program operates. Because there appears to be so much interest, we have created a new section in the Manual dealing with this topic. It is hoped that this information will help other groups or individuals. Please note the paragraphs in the **INTRODUCTION** which briefly describe the philosophy of our program.

By 1971, the human community in the Kalamazoo area had grown to the point where wildlife and people began to interact more frequently, particularly to the point where people were bringing more and more orphaned or injured animals to the Nature Center. At that time, the Nature Center had no organized program, nor did paid staff have the time or knowledge to deal with these animals. Two people began to care for the wildlife as volunteeers and began to recruit others to help when the load got too much to carry. From those early stages, the Rehabilitation Program grew to its present size and operating structure.

Currently (1987) the program has 74 trained volunteers in the community who help care for the more than 1,800 animals brought to the Nature Center each year.   The program is operated by the Wild Animal Rehabilitation Advisory Committee, which makes the policy and operational decisions; all Committee members are actively working in some phase of the Rehab Program.   The Advisory Committee is made up of 13 people, including one of the program's veterinarians and the Assistant Director of the Nature Center. Requirements for serving on the Committee are that members have served a minimum of 1 year as an active volunteer in the program and have demonstrated a clear interest in animals and a genuine commitment to active participation.   The Advisory Committee meets once a month; the officers are Chairman and Secretary.

STAFF

The Nature Center hires 3 part-time staff people during the most active time of the year to operate the office and program headquarters. From April 1 through August 31, the headquarters are manned 12:30-5:30 p.m. by paid, trained staff who answer phone calls on all manner of animal questions, receive all animals which are brought to the Center, examine animals for injuries or problems, keep animals warm and fed, call Rehab volunteers to come pick up various batches of animals, and keep records up to date and supplies in order. Staff also administer vaccinations under the supervision of licensed veterinarians who work with the program. No vaccines are sent home with volunteers. A part-time coordinator oversees the program, makes certain that communications are sent when necessary, and oversees staff. Volunteers assist staff in manning the Rehab office and answering the phone. Between September 1 and March 31, the program is operated by the part-time coordinator and members of the Advisory Committee who function to receive, examine, and place animals, communicate with program volunteers and the public, keep records, etc.

FACILITY

The Rehabilitation Program is located in the Interpretive Center of the Kalamazoo Nature Center in its own room. One large room serves as an intake facility, office, and holding area for animals waiting to be picked up by volunteers. It is hoped that one day the Rehab Program will have a larger facility. There are a number of large cages on the Nature Center property for release of those animals which are not sent home with volunteers--such as deer, fox, hawks and owls, badgers, or other unusual or large animals. A special pen has been constructed for deer next to a large horse barn so that stalls may be used if necessary. A long flight pen for release of raptors is located next to a stream and marsh and doubles as a pen for some of the raccoons when not in use otherwise. Five large cages at the Nature Center house permanently injured hawks, owls, and vultures which are used as parent birds or behavior models in raising young of those species. There are two pens for foxes on the Center's grounds and a holding and release pen for badgers. One aviary is used for release of songbirds or small hawks and owls on the grounds. Animal release pens have been built by volunteers on their own locations, and we plan to construct up to 10 transportable release pens.

FUNDING

Monies for the Wild Animal Rehabilitation Program come from several sources--donations by the public and people who bring animals to the program for treatment; interest income from an endowment fund (the Michael Albert Wild Animal Rehabilitation Fund); and monies from the Current Operating Fund of the Nature Center.

VETERINARIANS

The Nature Center is fortunate and grateful to have the services of Dr. Charles Mehne (Animal Clinic) and Dr. William Gregg (Bluegrass Animal Hospital) who donate their time, services, and drugs used for the animals in the program. Because it is important to be sensitive to the busy schedules and regular clients of the vets, every attempt is made to adapt to their schedules. One person within the Rehab Program serves as the liaison to the vets and handles all communications with them, schedules all appointments for animals which must be treated by the vets, takes most animals to the clinics, and sets up appointments with volunteers for animals which must be seen for re-checks after surgery or medication. Every attempt is made, at the request of the vets, to see that the only animals brought to them truly require their attention. Careful screening at the Rehab Office is necessary to make certain that those problems which trained staff or volunteers can handle are kept within the program personnel.

POLICY FOR ANIMALS GOING TO THE VETS

Out of concern for humane and appropriate treatment of animals and concern for maintaining a positive working relationship with our vets and the community, the following guidelines are adhered to by all staff and volunteers in the Wild Animal Rehabilitation Program.

A. Species which do not go to the vets under any circumstances--House Sparrows, starlings, pigeons, grackles and adult crossbred Mallard ducks.

B. Injuries--the following types of injuries that have little or no chance of success do not go to the vets.

    1. Birds with wings detached from the bone structure of the body, or wings broken at the shoulder or elbow joint. Birds with one broken

154

leg   may be taken because most birds can survive with one damaged
leg, provided that the good leg is not injured.

2. Mammals missing one or more limbs.

3. Animals severely diseased, emaciated or oozing severely from wounds,
    eyes, mouth; animals with broken back, neck, or crushed hips.

Deviation from this policy is only by special permission from appointed
Advisory Committee members.   Animals having any of the above types of
injuries will be euthanized as soon as possible after arrival at the office
out of respect for, and humane treatment of, the animal. Staff may tell the
public in a gentle but firm way that the animal's condition first must be
evaluated before we make a decision. Most people will understand that if an
animal is in pain and cannot be helped, the most humane thing to do is put
the animal out of its misery.

PERMITS
The Nature Center operates under both federal and state permits to possess
animals for scientific and rehabilitation purposes.   The Federal permit is
an extension of the Executive Director's permit for scientific and research
purposes, which was expanded to include wildlife rehabilitation.   The Center
also operates under the state of Michigan permit to "possess animals on a
temporary basis for wildlife rehabilitation."   Under state authorization the
Center also issues its own AUTHORIZATION PERMIT for each of its own
volunteers to possess animals for which the Center is responsible.
Accordingly, when each volunteer picks up a new batch of animals, he/she is
given a sheet of paper on Nature Center letterhead which states that the
volunteer may have possession of those animals for a specified time period
and that the batch of animals will be released by a specified time.
Volunteers are urged to keep these Authorization Permits in their possession
when holding or transporting animals. (See end of this chapter for a copy of
the permit.)   There are two volunteers in the Nature Center program who
operate within the program under their own Federal permits to possess raptors
and other birds for rehabilitation.

CLASSES

All volunteers are required to take the Wild Animal Rehabilitation class offered by experienced volunteers before they are allowed to accept animals. The class is offered twice in the spring, usually on a Saturday, and involves 6 hours of instruction in the raising and release of animals. Three hours of instruction are spent on all species of mammals, and 3 hours on all species of birds which the volunteers will likely take home to care for. A registration fee is charged to cover costs and includes a copy of the Manual for the volunteer. Volunteers indicate on a sign-up sheet their limitations in accepting animals--limitations such as allergies, work schedules, types of pens available for small or older animals, and special skills for particular species. A complete list of all volunteers, addresses, phone numbers, and limitations is mailed to everyone participating in the program so that they may get in touch with each other for help, information, or comfort. Children under 16 who wish to participate must be accompanied by and responsible to an adult in their immediate family. All policies and procedures are reviewed during the class. Experienced volunteers are encouraged to attend the classes for review and to share their ideas and techniques.

OTHER ASPECTS

One of the primary goals of the program is to educate the public as to what is truly an orphaned animal and what is a young baby out for its first exploring experiences. Phone callers are questioned to determine if an animal is healthy and calling for the adult. Young birds, feathered, hopping on the ground yet unable to fly, may have just been coaxed off the nest by the adult and will be located and fed if left alone. Callers are told to leave the area and allow adult mammals and birds to locate the young. If, after 12-24 hours, the young animal is still there, it is safe to assume that it is orphaned and only then is the caller encouraged to pick it up and bring it to the Center. People arriving at the Center with orphaned animals are questioned in the same manner, and, if the animal appears to belong back in the wild, staff advise these people to return quickly to the area in which the animal was found, leave it, and stay away for 12-24 hours. Callers are also told that it is illegal to possess wildlife without permits from the Department of Natural Resources. This helps discourage people from taking animals into their own homes and raising them incorrectly or imprinting them. If a caller must keep an animal overnight, basic temporary information is given on keeping the animal warm and hydrated with the warning that this is only overnight information and should not be used to try to raise the animal.

All wild Michigan animals, except bats or skunks, are accepted by the Rehabilitation Program including birds, mammals, reptiles, and amphibians provided that they are truly orphaned or injured. The Center cannot accept bats or skunks due to Department of Natural Resources restrictions for rabies control. All deer, fox, raptors, and badgers are kept on Nature Center grounds for raising and release. The Nature Center does not accept fall raccoons which have been raised by the public in their homes illegally. Rather, those people who discover that they do not want their raccoon any longer are informed about imprinting and urged to call the regional Department of Natural Resources office to discuss the situation. If they make a decision to try to release the animal, Rehab staff assist in directing them according to the **RELEASE** section in the **RACCOON** chapter.

———

For your reference we have included copies of the forms used in our program: ANIMAL DONATION intake, "hold harmless" form signed by the volunteer, temporary ANIMAL CARE AUTHORIZATION PERMIT, and "recognition of donation" by the volunteer. Please feel free to adopt what will assist you; however, please be certain that the forms you prepare comply with your local and state statutes as well as the federal ones.

The 2-part ANIMAL DONATION form is numbered sequentially. One part remains in the rehabilitation office while the second copy stays with the animal (whether with a volunteer or the veterinarian or as a specimen in the freezer). Sequentially numbered forms allow us to keep track of animals and help us to complete annual federal and state reports. Volunteers use their copies to account for disposition and success rate at the end of the season.

A temporary AUTHORIZATION PERMIT is prepared for every animal/litter and is given to the volunteer when he/she picks up the animal(s).

The "recognition of donation" form recognizes dollars spent by volunteers in the performance of their wild animal care and rehabilitation work. Volunteers may use this to verify income tax deductions.

KALAMAZOO Nature Center INC
FOR ENVIRONMENTAL EDUCATION
7000 N. Westnedge Avenue Kalamazoo, Michigan 49007
Telephone (616) 381-1574

ANIMAL DONATIONS

N⁰ 4353

DONOR: PLEASE FILL OUT TOP SECTION AS COMPLETELY AS POSSIBLE.

The Wild Animal Rehabilitation Program exists thanks to the generosity of our trained volunteers and your contributions. Our goal is to raise and release orphaned and injured wildlife to their rightful homes in nature. It costs approximately $10 for each bird and $25 for each mammal that we accept to rehabilitate. Your contributions are greatly needed and appreciated.

DONATION AMOUNT $_____

It is understood that in presenting this specimen to the Nature Center you waive all claim, title, and interest in this specimen and agree that the specimen shall become the sole property of the Kalamazoo Nature Center under the rules and regulations of the State of Michigan and the U.S. Fish and Wildlife Service.

Signature_____ Address_____
City, Zip_____ Phone_____ Date_____ Time_____

ANIMAL INFORMATION (Please be specific.)

Species_____ Number_____ Young_____ Adult_____

Condition: Orphaned____ When and where was the animal obtained--if different from
           Injured____ the above? Date_____ Time_____
           Dead____ Address or distance & direction from nearest intersection

Nature of Injury
_____ City_____ County_____ Twp._____
_____ How Obtained_____

Have you fed the animal(s)? No____ Yes____ If yes, what?_____
Medication? No____ Yes____ If yes, what?_____
Has the animal passed urine or feces in the last 24 hours? Yes____ No____ Unknown____

DISPOSITION (TO BE FILLED IN BY NATURE CENTER STAFF)

____Given to Wild Animal Care Volunteer   Name_____
                                 Date_____ Time_____
____Released   By_____ Date_____ Site_____
____Died   Nature of Death_____ Date_____
____Euthanized   Freezer Specimen_____ or Destroyed_____
____Held overnight at_____
____Unable to be released and held at_____
Name of Staff Member accepting the donation_____

FOR VETERINARIAN AND VOLUNTEER USE ONLY

Diagnosis_____
Prognosis_____
Treatment and recommendations_____
_____
Medication_____
Re-check date(s) and comments_____
Name of Veterinarian_____ Date_____

RACCOON AND FOX VACCINATIONS

FOR VOLUNTEERS WITH RACCOONS OR FOXES ONLY: PLEASE BRING IN YOUR RACCOON(S) OR FOX(ES) INTO THE REHAB. OFFICE ON THE FOLLOWING DATES FOR VACCINATIONS AND THE FIRST TWO WORMINGS.

Worming: Give first dosage when eyes open at 2-3 weeks. Give subsequent dosages every three weeks thereafter. 1 cc per 10 lbs.
         Dates_____/_____/_____/_____/_____/_____

Distemper: First shot given at 5 weeks of age. Date_____
             Second shot given 3 weeks later. Date_____

Rabies: First and only shot given at time of Date_____
          second distemper shot or when 8 weeks of age.

SERVING PEOPLE THROUGH EDUCATION, CONSERVATION, RESEARCH

MICS 1318 A report containing the percentage of charitable contributions expended by this organization on program, administration, and fund raising is available upon request.

158

KALAMAZOO NATURE CENTER
Wild Animal Care and Rehabilitation Program

Name_____

Birth date (Month/Year)_____

Address_____

City/ZIP_____

In consideration of your accepting my volunteer participation in the Wild Animal Care and Rehabilitation Program, I hereby for myself, my heirs, executors, administrators, and assigns, waive and release all claims for damages which I may have or which may hereafter accrue to me against the Kalamazoo Nature Center, its sponsors, agents, representatives, or assigns for any and all damages which may be sustained and suffered by me in connection with my association with or participation in the Wild Animal Care and Rehabilitation Program.

I acknowledge that I have been sufficiently informed by the Nature Center of the laws, rules, and regulations under which the program operates and that I will abide by those laws, rules, and regulations. I further acknowledge receipt of the Wild Animal Care and Rehabilitation Program policy manual and assume responsibility for knowledge of the information contained therein.

I have been informed of and understand the risks associated with rabies in wild animals. If an animal under my care inflicts an injury upon a human, I will report the incident to the Nature Center immediately and will abide by all pertinent policies and regulations. I have received a tetanus shot within the past 10 years and I understand that, in the event of an injury, I should receive a booster shot if it has been more than 5 years since my last tetanus shot.

I attest and verify that I have been sufficiently informed of the risks involved in the program and that I am physically fit and sufficiently trained to participate in this program.

Signature_____

Date_____

Parent or Guardian_____
(for person under 18 years of age)

KALAMAZOO

Nature Center INC.

FOR
ENVIRONMENTAL EDUCATION

7000 N. Westnedge Avenu
Kalamazoo, Michigan 490
Telephone (616) 381-157

TEMPORARY
ANIMAL CARE AUTHORIZATION PERMIT

This is to certify that _____ of

Name

_____

Address   City

is a qualified Animal Care Volunteer for the Kalamazoo Nature Center,
having completed a 6-hour training course, and is under the supervision
of professional staff members. This individual has in his/her care:

_____ _____, which temporarily legally belong(s)

No.   Species of Animal
to the Kalamazoo Nature Center and are/is covered by both State and
Federal permits. Said animal(s) will be cared for temporarily until

no later than _____, when it/they will be released in an

               Date
appropriate natural environment by Nature Center staff or a Wildlife
Care Volunteer, or returned to the Kalamazoo Nature Center for
permanent care.

Signed by

_____

Supervisor, Animal Care Program

_____

Assistant Director, Kalamazoo Nature Center

160

SERVING PEOPLE THROUGH EDUCATION, CONSERVATION, RESEARCH

MICS 1318 A report containing the percentage of charitable contributions expended by this organization on
program, administration, and fund raising is available upon request.

IT IS OUR UNDERSTANDING THAT

_____

HAS DONATED

$_____

TO THE KALAMAZOO NATURE CENTER'S
WILD ANIMAL CARE AND REHABILITATION PROGRAM.

Our sincere thank-you for all your
time and effort and for the above donation.

_____
H. Lewis Batts, Jr., Ph.D.
Executive Director
Kalamazoo Nature Center

_____
Date

_____
Patricia Adams, Coordinator
Wild Animal Care and Rehabilitation Program

SERVING PEOPLE THROUGH EDUCATION, CONSERVATION, RESEARCH

MICS 1318 A report containing the percentage of charitable contributions expended by this organization on
program, administration, and fund raising is available upon request.